I0701345

Mending *the* Adult Child *of* NARCISSISTS

The Art of Breaking Free, Healing Deep, and Living Fully

ALICE GLOVER

Mending the Adult Child of Narcissists

Copyright © 2024 by Alice Glover

All rights reserved. No part of this publication may be reproduced, distributed, or transmitted in any form or by any means, without the prior written permission of the publisher, except for brief quotations used in reviews or articles.

Published by True Pen Publishers

1234 Literary Lane

Fictionville, USA 54321

Phone: (555) 123-4567

Email: info@truepenpublishers.com

Website: www.truepenpublishers.com

Cover Design by: True Pen Publishers Design Team

Printed in the United States of America

Disclaimer: The information contained in this book is for general informational purposes only. While every effort has been made to ensure the accuracy of the content, the author and publisher assume no responsibility for any errors or omissions or for any consequences arising from the use of the information contained herein.

First Edition: 2024

Library of Congress Cataloging-in-Publication Data:

Taylor, Alexis Dawn. The Doomsday Prepping Survival Handbook for Novices.

Includes bibliographical references and index.

DEDICATION

To every adult child who has ever felt overshadowed, silenced, or unworthy. This book is for you. May you find the courage to heal, the strength to reclaim your life, and the joy of discovering your true self. Your journey is valid, your pain is real, and your future is bright.

ACKNOWLEDGEMENT

This book has been a labor of love, and it would not have been possible without the support and encouragement of many incredible individuals.

To my family and friends, who have been my anchors and sounding boards throughout this journey. Your unwavering belief in me has been my greatest motivation.

To the countless individuals who have shared their stories with me—your vulnerability and resilience have inspired every word of this book. Thank you for trusting me with your experiences.

To the professionals and experts in the fields of psychology and self-help, whose research and insights have enriched this work. Your dedication to understanding and healing the human psyche is truly remarkable.

To my editors and publishing team, for your meticulous attention to detail and your unwavering commitment to bringing this book to life. Your expertise has been invaluable.

Finally, to you, the reader. Thank you for taking this brave step toward healing and self discovery. May this book be a source of strength, hope, and transformation for you.

With heartfelt gratitude.

PREFACE

Welcome to "Mending the Adult Child of Narcissists." If you're here, it's likely because you've experienced the tumultuous waves of growing up with a narcissistic parent. You may have found yourself doubting your worth, grappling with guilt, and struggling to define who you are without the ever-present shadow of manipulation and criticism. This book is for you—an invitation to embark on a profound journey of healing and self-discovery.

As a child of a narcissistic parent, you've faced invisible battles that many around you may never understand. The constant need for validation, the fear of rejection, and the nagging voice of an internal critic can all be traced back to the complex dynamics of your upbringing. It's a harsh reality that often leaves deep, unseen scars. But it's also a reality that you can overcome.

In the pages that follow, we'll delve into the intricate web of narcissistic parenting and its enduring impact. We'll explore the emotional landscape of guilt, shame, and self-doubt that you've navigated for so long. You'll learn to identify the toxic patterns that hold you back, set boundaries that protect your well-being, and find the strength to say "no" without guilt.

This book isn't just about understanding the past; it's about reclaiming your future. You'll discover how to nurture yourself emotionally, build healthier relationships, and pursue your passions without seeking external validation. We'll walk you through daily practices for emotional health, and help you connect with supportive communities that uplift and inspire you.

Healing from the wounds of a narcissistic upbringing is not a linear journey. There will be setbacks and moments of doubt, but each step forward is a victory. This book is designed to be your companion through these ups and downs, providing insights, tools, and encouragement to help you stay strong and resilient.

"Mending the Adult Child of Narcissists" is not just a guide; it's a lifeline. It's a testament to your courage and resilience, and a roadmap to a future where you can live authentically, embrace your true self, and find peace. Your story matters, and your healing is possible. Let's embark on this journey together.

TABLE OF CONTENTS

INTRODUCTION

You're Not Alone in This Journey

Why This Book Is for You

If you're reading this, chances are you've spent a lot of time feeling like something about your upbringing wasn't quite right. Maybe you've struggled with feelings of inadequacy, guilt, or self-doubt that just won't seem to go away. Perhaps relationships—whether with family, friends, or romantic partners—feel like a minefield, full of invisible triggers and unspoken expectations. Or maybe you've reached a point where you're simply tired of carrying the emotional baggage that seems to follow you everywhere.

Whatever brought you here, let me start by saying this: **You are not alone, and your pain is valid.**

Growing up with a narcissistic parent isn't something most people talk about openly. It's a silent wound, often hidden behind a mask of "I turned out fine" or "It wasn't that bad." But deep down, you know the truth. You know what it's like to feel unseen, unheard, and unworthy. You know what it's like to tiptoe around someone's moods, to second-guess your feelings, and to wonder if you're the problem.

Let me be clear: **You are not the problem.**

The problem lies in the dynamics you were raised in—the constant need to cater to someone else's ego, the shifting goalposts of approval, and the emotional neglect or manipulation that left you questioning your worth. These experiences weren't your fault, and they don't define you.

This book is for you if:

- You've ever felt like no matter what you do, it's never good enough.

- You struggle with boundaries because saying "no" feels like a betrayal.

- You find yourself drawn to relationships that mimic the chaos or control of your childhood.

- You carry a deep sense of guilt or shame that you can't quite explain.

- You want to heal, but you're not sure where to start.

Healing is possible. It's not easy, and it won't happen overnight, but it's worth it. You deserve to live a life free from the shadows of your past, and this book is here to guide you on that journey.

What You'll Find Here

Clarity for the Chaos

One of the hardest parts of growing up with a narcissistic parent is making sense of what happened. Narcissistic abuse is often subtle and insidious—it's not always the outright yelling or neglect you see in movies. It's the offhand comments that make you doubt yourself, the unspoken rules that keep you walking on eggshells, the constant sense that your needs don't matter as much as theirs.

This book will help you understand these dynamics. You'll learn about the traits of narcissistic parents, how their behavior affects children, and why it's not your fault. We'll break down complex psychological concepts into plain language, so you can finally put a name to the feelings and patterns you've been struggling with.

A Toolkit for Healing

Understanding is the first step, but healing requires action. That's why this book is packed with practical tools to help you move forward. You'll learn how to:

- Recognize and challenge the negative beliefs you've internalized.

- Set healthy boundaries that protect your peace.

- Reconnect with your authentic self—the "you" that existed before the pain.

- Build healthier relationships based on trust and mutual respect.

- Develop self-compassion and embrace the idea that you are enough.

Each chapter includes reflective exercises to help you process what you've learned and apply it to your life. Whether it's journaling prompts, thought experiments, or simple action steps, these exercises are designed to meet you where you are and move you closer to where you want to be.

Healing can feel lonely, but you're not the only one walking this path. Throughout the book, you'll find real-life stories from people who've faced similar struggles and come out stronger on the other side. These stories aren't just here to inspire you—they're here to remind you that progress is possible, no matter how stuck you feel right now.

This book isn't about blaming your parents or dwelling on the past. It's about understanding what happened so you can break free from its grip. Whether you're still in contact with your parent, have gone no-contact, or are somewhere in between, this book respects your choices. There's no right or wrong way to navigate these relationships—only what feels right for you.

How to Use This Book

Healing is a deeply personal journey, and there's no one-size-fits-all approach. That's why this book is structured to let you move at your own pace.

Take It Step by Step

The chapters are organized into three parts:

1. **Untangling the Past:** Understanding how your upbringing shaped you.

2. **Breaking Free from Old Patterns:** Learning practical strategies to reclaim your power and rebuild your self-esteem.

3. **Creating a Life You Love:** Building a future that's not defined by your past.

Each chapter builds on the last, but feel free to skip around if something resonates with you more urgently. This is your journey—take it in whatever order makes sense for you.

Engage with the Exercises

At the end of each chapter, you'll find reflective exercises designed to deepen your understanding and help you take actionable steps toward healing. These aren't just "homework"—they're opportunities to connect with yourself and process your experiences in a safe and meaningful way.

For example, you might find prompts like:

- "Write about a time you felt dismissed by your parent. How does that experience still affect you today?"

- "List three ways you've been kind to yourself this week. If you haven't, what's one small act of kindness you can do for yourself right now?"

These exercises are tools to help you turn insight into action. The more you engage with them, the more progress you'll see.

The personal stories in this book are here to remind you that you're not alone. If you ever feel overwhelmed or stuck, let these stories be a source of hope and connection. They're proof that healing is possible, even when it feels out of reach.

Some parts of this book might challenge you. That's okay. Growth often feels uncomfortable at first, especially when you're unpacking deep wounds. Give yourself permission to take breaks, revisit sections, or sit with your emotions as they come up. This is a journey, not a race.

As you turn the page, I want you to take a moment to honor the courage it took to pick up this book. Seeking help, asking questions, and exploring your pain are acts of bravery. You're here because you want something better for yourself, and that desire is the first step toward healing.

The path ahead won't always be easy, but it will be worth it. And you don't have to walk it alone. This book is your companion, your guide, and your reminder that you are capable of growth, love, and joy.

UNTANGLING THE PAST

*Why You Feel the Way You Do—and How to
Start Moving Forward*

Chapter 1

What Growing Up with a Narcissist Does to You

"You are never enough, but I am everything."

This sentence might sound like an exaggeration, but if you grew up with a narcissistic parent, you've probably heard something similar, either in words or through their actions. The constant need for validation, the endless manipulation, and the unsettling feeling that nothing you did ever quite measured up—it shapes the way you see yourself and the world around you. It can feel like you were raised in a world where your needs didn't matter, and where the emotional landscape was one of instability, confusion, and endless self-doubt.

If any of this resonates with you, you're not alone.

Growing up with a narcissistic parent is a unique kind of pain. You may have spent your childhood walking on eggshells, trying to meet impossible standards, and yearning for the kind of love and attention that seemed to always be just out of reach. In a household like this, love often feels conditional—based on what you can do for them, how well you perform, or how much you can boost their ego. And when you inevitably fall short, as children often do, the emotional fallout can be devastating.

The purpose of this chapter is simple: to give you clarity. We're going to shed light on the deep psychological impacts of having a narcissistic parent. We'll explore how this upbringing affects your emotional and psychological wellbeing, and, most importantly, we'll validate your experiences. It's time to stop questioning whether your pain is real or if you're somehow imagining things. If you grew up with a narcissistic parent, you've been carrying invisible wounds, and it's okay to acknowledge them. Your feelings are real. Your struggles are valid. And you are not the only one carrying this weight.

I know it can be overwhelming to realize just how much of your current emotional struggles trace back to your upbringing. Maybe you've struggled with self-esteem for as long as you can remember. Or perhaps relationships have always felt challenging, and you've found yourself caught in toxic patterns that leave you feeling drained and confused. You might feel like something's "off," but you're not sure where it all started. This chapter will help you understand that the roots of your struggles run deep. But knowing where the pain came from is the first step toward healing.

Let's start by understanding what narcissism really means, because it's more than just being selfish or egotistical. Narcissism, in its clinical sense, refers to a personality disorder where a person has an inflated sense of self-importance, a lack of empathy, and a constant need for admiration and validation. In the case of narcissistic parents, these traits often manifest as emotional neglect, manipulation, and control. Instead of providing nurturing, unconditional love, a narcissistic parent uses their child to fulfill their own emotional needs, often without any regard for the child's well-being. Their love is conditional, only given when the child behaves in a way that reflects well on the parent or boosts their ego.

You may have been the object of their manipulation—forced to take care of their emotional needs, while your own were ignored. Perhaps you found yourself in the impossible position of having to parent your parent, a role reversal that robbed you of the childhood you deserved. You may have felt like a pawn in their game of emotional chess, where your worth was constantly tied to how well you reflected their image or fulfilled their needs.

This chapter is not about blaming your parent or making them out to be a villain. It's about understanding how their behaviors shaped your emotional landscape and how you can begin to heal from the long-lasting effects of that upbringing. Narcissistic parents can be difficult to understand because they can also be charming, talented, and even loving in their own way—on their terms. But those who grew up in their shadow know that their love comes with conditions, and it often feels like a bargain rather than a gift.

There are a few key themes we'll explore in this chapter:

1. **The Behaviors of Narcissistic Parents:** We'll take a close look at what narcissism looks like in parenting. How does a narcissistic parent behave? What are the subtle (and not-so-subtle) ways they manipulate, control, and emotionally neglect their children? These behaviors often leave scars that last a lifetime, and understanding them is the first step toward healing.

2. **The Emotional and Psychological Wounds:** We'll talk about the emotional toll growing up with

a narcissistic parent takes on you. From chronic feelings of guilt and shame to low self-esteem and difficulty trusting others, the scars run deep. These emotional wounds aren't your fault, but they've shaped the way you see yourself and the world. We'll explore how these wounds manifest in your adult life and why they are so hard to heal.

3. **The Myths About Narcissistic Families:** There are many misconceptions about what it means to grow up with a narcissistic parent. People may think that narcissistic parents are always overtly abusive, or that their children just need to "get over it." But the truth is that narcissistic parenting can be insidious—hidden behind the façade of love, success, or normalcy. You may have been told that your experiences weren't as bad as others' or that you should be grateful for what you had. This chapter will debunk those myths and help you understand that your pain is real, no matter how it looked on the outside.

This chapter is just the beginning. As you read, I encourage you to reflect on your own experiences. The goal here is to gain insight into how your upbringing shaped your emotional world, so you can begin to understand the patterns that have followed you into adulthood. Your story is unique, but I promise you—if you grew up with a narcissistic parent, you are not alone. And together, we'll begin to heal the wounds that have held you back for far too long.

In the next chapter, we'll dive deeper into the emotions that come with growing up in a narcissistic household—feelings of guilt, shame, and confusion—and begin the process of learning how to manage and heal from them. But for now, take a deep breath and allow yourself to acknowledge what you've been through. You've already taken the most important step in your healing journey—recognizing that your experiences matter and that you deserve to heal.

The Narcissistic Parent Playbook

At the heart of narcissistic parenting is the overwhelming need for control. A narcissistic parent views the world through a lens that revolves around their own needs, desires, and insecurities. This might look like an insistence that everything must go their way—whether it's how the house is organized, how family events unfold, or even how you behave. You might have grown up walking on eggshells, constantly adjusting your actions, moods, and decisions to avoid setting off your parent's anger or disappointment.

Example: Maybe you recall an incident where you wanted to spend time with friends, but your narcissistic parent became upset because they felt you were "abandoning" them. They might have said something like, "I guess I'm not as important as your friends" or "You never care about me." These comments weren't about you; they were about your parent's need to control your actions, your time, and, ultimately, your sense of worth.

This need for control often extends beyond the big moments. It can show up in smaller, everyday ways: choosing what you wear, dictating how you should feel about certain things, or pushing their own opinions as facts. The narcissistic parent doesn't just want to be in charge—they want to define everything in your life to make themselves feel secure and important.

Manipulation and Emotional Control

Narcissistic parents often use manipulation as a way to maintain control. They excel at making you feel guilty or responsible for their emotions, which puts you in a constant state of self-doubt and guilt. They might manipulate your feelings to create a sense of obligation or to silence your needs.

Example: Picture a scenario where your narcissistic parent, when confronted about their behavior, might say something like, "After all I've done for you, this is how you repay me?" This tactic is designed to make you feel guilty for expressing any unhappiness or discomfort. Instead of addressing the real issue at hand, the narcissist flips the script, putting the emotional burden squarely on your shoulders.

They might also use "love" as a bargaining chip. A narcissistic parent may shower you with praise when you're doing what they want, only to withdraw that affection when you don't meet their expectations. This creates an unpredictable emotional landscape that keeps you hooked in the cycle of seeking their approval. The love they give can feel conditional and inconsistent, making you unsure of where you stand emotionally.

Example: One day, your narcissistic parent might praise you for an accomplishment, saying, "I'm so proud of you—this is just what I expected." But the next day, they could turn cold, saying, "Why didn't you do better? This isn't good enough." This emotional whiplash leaves you constantly chasing approval, unsure of what will make them happy, and questioning your worth.

The Lack of Empathy: How It Affects Your Emotional World

One of the most painful aspects of growing up with a narcissistic parent is the emotional neglect that often accompanies their behavior. Narcissistic parents tend to lack empathy—they are unable or unwilling to see the world from your perspective. As a result, your emotions and needs are frequently ignored or dismissed. You might have experienced this as feeling invisible or unimportant in your own home.

Example: Perhaps you remember an instance when you were upset about something, and instead of offering comfort, your parent told you to "stop being dramatic" or "get over it." Your feelings were invalidated, and you were left alone with your pain. This emotional neglect can lead to deep feelings of loneliness, even when you're surrounded by others.

In extreme cases, the narcissistic parent may also belittle your emotions as a way to control them. If you were sad, they might accuse you of being weak or ungrateful. If you were happy, they might try to bring you down with criticism. Either way, your emotional experience was never fully seen, heard, or valued.

The Need for Admiration: Projecting Insecurities onto You

A key feature of narcissistic parenting is the constant need for admiration. Narcissistic parents seek validation from those around them, and often, that need is projected onto their children. You may have been treated like an extension of your parent's ego rather than as an individual with your own needs and desires. Your achievements may have been celebrated, but only when they served to boost your parent's self-esteem or image.

Example: You might have experienced moments where your parent insisted that your achievements were a reflection of their greatness. "Look at what I did! I raised such a smart child," they might have said, disregarding your own hard work and accomplishments. This subtly undermines your sense of self-worth, leaving you to wonder if your achievements were ever truly yours—or just a way for your parent to get attention.

The narcissistic parent doesn't see their children as individuals but as tools to meet their emotional needs. This can lead to a lifetime of feeling like you're only valued for what you can give to someone else, rather than being seen for who you truly are.

How Narcissistic Behavior Works

So, why do narcissistic parents act this way? At the core of narcissism is a fragile sense of self. Narcissistic parents project their own insecurities and unmet emotional needs onto their children because they struggle with feelings of inadequacy or low self-worth. Rather than confronting their own vulnerabilities, they manipulate and control their environment to maintain a sense of superiority and power.

This behavior often stems from early childhood experiences where the narcissistic parent may have faced emotional neglect, trauma, or a lack of validation themselves. Instead of developing healthy coping mechanisms, they learn to rely on control and manipulation to feel secure. Unfortunately, this pattern is passed on to their children, often leaving them trapped in a cycle of emotional turmoil.

The Invisible Wounds

Growing up with a narcissistic parent is like living in a world where your needs, feelings, and even your very existence often seem to take a backseat to someone else's ego. This creates wounds that aren't visible to the eye—

wounds that don't leave scars on the skin but cut deeply into the soul. These wounds, the invisible ones, are often the hardest to identify and even harder to heal. Yet, they are the ones that shape how you see yourself and the world around you, long after you leave home.

As a child of a narcissistic parent, you were likely made to feel that you were never "good enough." No matter how hard you tried, your achievements were either dismissed or overshadowed by the parent's own inflated sense of importance. If you succeeded, it was never your own accomplishment—it was because you did something that reflected well on them. If you failed, it was proof that you were inadequate. In either case, you were left to wonder who you were beyond their expectations and demands.

The Emotional and Psychological Toll

The emotional toll of this upbringing can be profound. One of the most common and crushing experiences for the adult child of a narcissist is feeling unloved and invalidated. Narcissistic parents often lack the capacity for genuine empathy, and as a result, their children rarely receive the emotional validation they need to develop a healthy sense of self. Your emotions were either ignored or trivialized, leaving you with the unsettling sense that your feelings didn't matter. This kind of emotional neglect isn't just about not being loved—it's about being made to feel that love was conditional upon how well you met their needs and expectations.

This creates an insidious cycle of chronic self-doubt. If your emotions were dismissed or belittled, you were forced to second-guess your own thoughts and feelings. You learned to doubt your own worth, constantly wondering if you were simply too much, too sensitive, or too flawed to be truly loved. You may have felt like you had to apologize for your existence, constantly walking on eggshells, fearing that the slightest mistake would lead to rejection or punishment. Even if your parent was outwardly "nice" at times, you couldn't escape the underlying message that your worth was tied to their mood or approval.

Over time, this sense of being "not enough" becomes a toxic inner narrative that can be hard to shake. It whispers to you in quiet moments, telling you that you don't deserve happiness or success, and that you're forever unworthy of love. This is the legacy of narcissistic parenting: a deep and lasting wound to your self-esteem.

But these invisible wounds don't just stay locked inside you—they shape your behavior, too. They can influence how you relate to others, how you make decisions, and even how you see yourself in the world.

The Long-Term Effects on Behavior and Relationships

One of the most common outcomes of growing up with a narcissistic parent is difficulty in forming healthy relationships. In your childhood, your emotional needs were either ignored or manipulated, which leaves you unsure of what healthy emotional connections look like. As an adult, you may struggle with trusting others or with being truly vulnerable in relationships. This is because you were never taught what it meant to be loved unconditionally or to receive genuine support and care. Your relationships may be built on the distorted belief that love is earned through pleasing others or by being perfect. You might constantly worry about being rejected or abandoned, just as you were by your narcissistic parent.

Take Rachel, for example. She grew up in a home where her mother's needs always came first. Her accomplishments were never celebrated unless they made her mother look good. When Rachel graduated from college with honors, her mother simply commented, "Well, it's about time." Over time, Rachel learned to suppress her own needs and desires in order to avoid conflict and gain her mother's approval. As an adult, she found herself in relationships where she continually overcompensated for others, trying to fix their problems and please them at the expense of her own happiness. She became a classic "people-pleaser," always afraid of rejection if she said no or expressed her true feelings.

The feeling of "not being good enough" can also lead to perfectionism. As a child, you learned that your worth was conditional on meeting certain standards—standards that were often unreasonable or unattainable. This drives you as an adult to constantly strive for perfection, believing that only by achieving the highest possible standard can you finally prove your worth. But no matter how much you achieve, it never feels like enough, and the sense of inadequacy lingers.

David's story illustrates this struggle. Growing up with a narcissistic father who demanded perfection, David became obsessed with achieving success in his career. He believed that if he were just successful enough, his father would finally acknowledge him. But even after landing a high-paying job and being recognized for his achievements, his father's praise was sparse and fleeting. No matter what David did, it was never enough. He felt empty inside, constantly chasing approval that would never come, and his relationships suffered as a result. He found it difficult to trust that people loved him for who he was, not for what he could do for them.

Emotional Neglect and the Unseen Damage

At the core of these invisible wounds is the concept of **emotional neglect**. Emotional neglect is often overlooked because it isn't as obvious as physical abuse or verbal attacks. But the long-term effects can be just as damaging. Narcissistic parents fail to provide the emotional care that a child needs to develop a healthy sense of self. They don't nurture their child's emotional growth because their own needs are always prioritized. This leaves the child to fend for themselves emotionally, often without the tools or support they need to navigate their feelings.

For example, a child of a narcissistic parent may not learn how to manage their emotions or how to express vulnerability. They may grow up feeling emotionally "disconnected," unsure of how to regulate their feelings or process difficult emotions like sadness, anger, or fear. This can lead to emotional dysregulation as an adult, where even minor stresses can feel overwhelming and uncontrollable. Many adult children of narcissists also struggle with feelings of isolation because they learned early on that their emotional needs weren't important enough to warrant attention.

Myths About Narcissistic Families

There are several myths and misconceptions about narcissistic families that can make it harder for you to make sense of your experiences. In this section, we're going to tackle these myths head-on and provide some much-needed validation for what you've gone through.

Myth #1: "All Parents Have Their Child's Best Interests at Heart"

One of the most pervasive myths is that all parents, no matter how flawed, have their child's best interests in mind. This idea is comforting because it implies that parents inherently love and care for their children, and that any shortcomings are merely the result of stress, ignorance, or bad circumstances. While it's true that many parents do their best, this myth doesn't apply in the case of narcissistic parenting. Narcissistic parents often operate from a deeply self-centered place, and their primary concern is their own needs, desires, and emotional regulation—not the well-being of their children.

For a narcissistic parent, their child is often seen as an extension of themselves, existing to validate their self-worth. This means that the child is expected to reflect the parent's desires and maintain the parent's image of superiority. If the child's behavior, needs, or emotions don't align with the narcissistic parent's expectations, the child may face neglect, emotional abuse, or manipulation. For example, if a narcissistic parent is upset because their child didn't perform well at school, rather than comforting the child, they might lash out, saying things like, "You're ruining my reputation" or "I can't believe how selfish you are."

This self-centered approach to parenting can be incredibly damaging because it denies the child the emotional support and validation they need to develop a healthy sense of self. It also leads to a constant feeling of being used or unloved, as the child is never seen for who they truly are, but only for how they serve the narcissistic parent's needs.

Myth #2: "Children Exaggerate Their Parents' Faults"

Another myth often perpetuated about narcissistic families is the idea that children exaggerate their parents' faults or create stories to make their upbringing seem worse than it actually was. This myth can be particularly harmful because it silences the child's truth, making them feel like their experiences are invalid or not important enough to be taken seriously. It implies that if the parent says they love their child or tries to apologize, then the child should forget the past and move on.

The truth is that narcissistic abuse is insidious. It's often subtle and hidden behind a mask of charm, manipulation, or promises of love. Narcissistic parents are experts at gaslighting—twisting reality and making their children question their own perceptions. If a child speaks out about the emotional neglect, the cruel comments, or the manipulative behavior they endured, they may be told, "You're being too sensitive," or "That never happened. You're just remembering it wrong." Over time, this constant invalidation can cause the child to doubt their own memory and perception, leading them to believe that maybe they *are* exaggerating or making things up.

However, the emotional scars left by narcissistic abuse are very real, and the pain is not something that should be dismissed or minimized. It's important to recognize that just because a parent has moments of kindness or offers occasional praise doesn't erase the emotional manipulation, control, or neglect that may also be present. It's not an exaggeration—it's a reflection of the emotional chaos that comes with narcissistic parenting.

Myth #3: "Friends and Family Would Understand if You Just Told Them"

Another painful myth is the belief that if you just explain your experience to others—like friends, extended family, or even therapists—they'll immediately understand and support you. Unfortunately, narcissistic abuse is so emotionally complex and often hidden beneath the surface that it can be difficult for people outside of the situation to comprehend. This is especially true for those who have not experienced narcissistic parenting themselves.

Narcissistic parents often present a charming, well-put-together front to the outside world, making it hard for anyone else to see the dysfunction beneath. They may act like the perfect parent when other people are around, but behind closed doors, they may be emotionally neglectful, controlling, or even abusive. For outsiders, this can lead to confusion or disbelief when a child tries to explain the situation. Friends or family might say, "Your parent always seemed so nice," or "They're not that bad," not understanding the covert and manipulative nature of narcissistic behavior.

This lack of understanding can leave the adult child feeling incredibly isolated. It can create feelings of shame, as if they're the only ones who have experienced this kind of treatment or that somehow they're at fault for not having a better relationship with their parent. It's important to acknowledge that this external doubt isn't about you—it's about the complexity of narcissistic abuse and how it's often misunderstood by those who haven't lived through it.

Myth #4: "Your Pain Is Not as Bad as You Think"

Finally, one of the most damaging myths is the belief that the pain caused by narcissistic parenting is not as severe as it feels. This myth can arise from people who haven't experienced narcissistic abuse, and it often comes in the form of well-meaning but misguided advice. Phrases like, "You're an adult now—just move on" or "Other people have it worse" can make you feel like your emotional struggles are not worthy of attention or care.

The reality is that the effects of narcissistic parenting can be profound and long-lasting. Emotional abuse, neglect, and manipulation can create deep wounds that affect how you see yourself, how you relate to others, and how you navigate the world. The pain you feel is real, and it deserves to be recognized, validated, and healed. Just because others may not fully understand or appreciate the depth of your pain doesn't make it any less real.

Reassurance and Validation

It's crucial to remember that your experiences are valid, and your pain is legitimate. The myths surrounding narcissistic families only serve to invalidate your reality, but the truth is, growing up with a narcissistic parent leaves deep emotional scars. You didn't imagine the manipulation, the control, or the emotional neglect. And even if others don't understand, your feelings are real, and your journey toward healing matters.

As you continue through this book, I want you to know that you are not alone. Your story is valid, and there is hope for healing and recovery. With the right tools, support, and understanding, you can break free from the patterns of narcissistic abuse and create a life where you are free to be your true, authentic self. Your pain does not define you, and healing is not just possible—it's waiting for you.

Reflective Exercise

"Write a letter to your younger self. What do you want them to know about the love and support they deserved?"

____

____

____

____

____

Chapter 2

The Feelings That Won't Let Go

Imagine for a moment waking up each day with a heavy, invisible burden on your chest. It's a weight that doesn't come from your circumstances, but from inside—buried deep in your heart and mind. It's the lingering feeling of **guilt**, the quiet voice in your head that tells you you're never enough. It's the sting of **shame**, the belief that something is inherently wrong with you. These emotions feel like old friends you never invited, but they've been with you for so long, you can't imagine life without them.

Does this sound familiar? If you grew up with a narcissistic parent, you probably know exactly what I mean. The emotional aftermath of living with narcissistic abuse isn't always obvious—it doesn't always leave visible scars, but it **lingers**. It shapes the way you view yourself, others, and the world around you. It's one of the reasons why healing from such an upbringing can feel so overwhelming: these emotions often feel like they've been with you forever, following you through every stage of your adult life.

This chapter is all about **understanding these emotions—guilt**, **shame**, and the subtle manipulation tactics like **gaslighting** that make it all the more confusing. We'll dive deep into why these feelings stick to you like glue, how they distort your sense of self, and why it's so crucial to finally allow yourself the **space to grieve**. If you've been carrying this emotional baggage, know that you're not alone, and it's time to start unpacking it.

The Emotion That Feels Like a Heavy Blanket: Guilt

Guilt is a powerful force when you grow up with a narcissistic parent. It's often the first thing you feel when things go wrong, and it's the last thing you let go of. But what's behind this constant sense of guilt?

In a narcissistic household, love and approval often come with strings attached. You were probably conditioned to believe that **everything you did was for someone else's approval**, and no matter how hard you tried, it was never enough. Your achievements were either ignored or criticized, and your mistakes were magnified. That's because, for a narcissistic parent, **your existence was about their needs, not yours**. When you didn't meet those needs, you were made to feel guilty for simply being yourself.

This kind of guilt is insidious because it doesn't just go away as you grow older—it becomes a default emotional state. You feel guilty when you prioritize your own needs over others, guilty when you say no, guilty when you speak up. You might even feel guilty when you don't feel guilty, because you've been trained to believe you're responsible for everyone's feelings. This guilt may have grown so deeply rooted in your life that you don't even notice how it's affecting your choices today.

But here's the truth: **You are not responsible for someone else's emotional well-being**, especially not your narcissistic parent. This guilt you're carrying? It's theirs, not yours.

Shame: The Voice in Your Head That Tells You You're Not Enough

Shame is another emotion that sticks to you like a shadow. Unlike guilt, which can be about specific actions or behaviors, shame goes deeper. It's not just about what you did or didn't do—it's about who you are at your core.

If you grew up with a narcissistic parent, chances are you were often made to feel like you were **never enough**. You were criticized for your personality, your achievements, your appearance—nothing you did was ever good enough for them. You were either **too much** or **not enough**, but never exactly right.

Over time, this constant criticism chips away at your sense of self. You internalize these messages until you believe that something is inherently wrong with you. Maybe you start to feel like you're **unlovable** or **defective**, and that nobody could ever truly care about you. These feelings of shame are often unconscious, so you may not even realize how much they affect the way you see yourself and the choices you make. You might have a tendency to overcompensate, to please others, to hide your true feelings—anything to avoid the uncomfortable belief that you're not enough.

The truth is that **shame is a lie**. It tells you that you are broken or unworthy of love, but that couldn't be further from the truth. What happened to you wasn't your fault. The shame you feel was **imposed upon you** by a parent who couldn't see your worth.

Gaslighting: The Power of Doubt

If you've ever been told that you're "too sensitive" or "making things up" when you try to express your emotions or experiences, you've probably encountered **gaslighting**. Gaslighting is a form of psychological manipulation that makes you question your own reality. It's a tactic narcissistic parents often use to control and diminish their children's sense of self.

You may have been told that your feelings weren't valid, that you were **overreacting**, or that you misunderstood what happened. Over time, this constant doubt can make you question everything about yourself, even your memories. You might even start to feel like you can't trust your own perception of reality.

The danger of gaslighting is that it **disconnects you from your truth**. It makes you doubt your own experiences, which only deepens the emotional wounds. If you've been gaslighted, it's not your fault. The narcissist used this tactic to maintain control and avoid accountability for their actions.

Grieving for the Childhood You Didn't Have

Another important step in this chapter is **grieving**—grieving for the childhood you never had. It's a process that many people overlook, but it's vital for healing. You never had the chance to experience **healthy love**,

validation, and support because those things were withheld or manipulated by your narcissistic parent.

This grief can show up in many ways—**sadness**, **anger**, or even feelings of emptiness. But it's crucial to allow yourself to feel this grief and acknowledge the loss of the healthy, loving environment you deserved. Healing starts when you **give yourself permission to mourn** for the parent-child relationship you never had.

Why Guilt and Shame Feel Like Home

Imagine this: You're a child, sitting at the dinner table, eagerly awaiting your parent's praise for the art project you've spent hours on. You've put so much of yourself into it, hoping they'll see your effort. When you show it to them, you're met with silence, maybe a brief glance, and then a cutting remark like, "It's not even that good," or "You could've done better."

In that moment, the excitement you felt about your accomplishment fades, replaced by a sinking feeling in your stomach. You begin to question your worth, your abilities, and your very sense of self. You know something isn't right, but you don't have the words to explain it. Instead, you internalize the experience, believing that maybe, just maybe, you're the problem. Maybe you're just not enough.

As an adult, those feelings might still linger—long after the art project is forgotten. You might find yourself questioning your every move, apologizing unnecessarily, or constantly seeking approval from others. **Guilt** and **shame** have followed you into adulthood, making it hard to shake the belief that you're somehow flawed, unworthy, or constantly falling short.

How Guilt and Shame Become Ingrained

This scenario is familiar to many adult children of narcissistic parents. Guilt and shame are often the primary tools used by narcissistic parents to maintain control over their children. Unlike typical parenting, where love and support serve as a foundation for development, narcissistic parents create an environment where validation is conditional. In these households, children are often left wondering, *"What do I need to do to make them proud? Will I ever be enough?"* The need for approval becomes a constant cycle, but no matter how much you give or how hard you try, it's never enough.

Narcissistic parents tend to see their children not as individuals with their own needs and emotions but as extensions of themselves. If the child fails to meet their parent's expectations or behaves in a way that doesn't align with the parent's image of perfection, the response is often harsh and punitive. They might use guilt to manipulate, saying things like, *"After all I've done for you, this is how you repay me?"* or *"You've ruined everything for me."* These phrases implant the belief that the child is the source of the parent's unhappiness, leading them to internalize feelings of guilt, even when the situation has nothing to do with them.

Shame is another emotional weapon frequently used by narcissistic parents. While guilt focuses on what the child has done (or not done), shame focuses on who the child is. Narcissistic parents often criticize their children for their very being, telling them they're not good enough, that they'll never live up to their potential, or even worse, making them feel invisible or unimportant. This constant invalidation teaches the child that they are inherently flawed—that there's something wrong with them at their core.

The Long-Term Effects of Guilt and Shame

As a child, you may have learned to hide your emotions or avoid expressing your true feelings, afraid of being criticized or belittled. Over time, this teaches you that your feelings are wrong, invalid, or too much. This conditioning creates deep emotional wounds that can manifest as chronic feelings of guilt and shame throughout adulthood. These emotions, while originating in childhood, become deeply rooted and can influence many aspects of life.

One of the most significant effects of growing up in an environment filled with guilt and shame is its impact on **self-esteem**. When a child is repeatedly told they're not enough, they begin to believe it. This belief doesn't just go away with age—it lingers in adulthood, affecting how they view themselves and their abilities. The voice of the narcissistic parent becomes an inner critic, constantly reminding them that they aren't worthy of love, success, or happiness. They might feel like they have to work harder, do more, or be perfect in order to gain the approval they've been deprived of. This often leads to feelings of being "never good enough," no matter how much they achieve or how hard they try.

Another area where guilt and shame take a toll is in **decision-making**. The chronic self-doubt that stems from these emotions often leads to paralysis when it comes to making choices. In relationships, work, and even personal goals, you might find yourself second-guessing your every decision, worried that you'll make the wrong choice or upset someone in the process. The fear of making a mistake and facing judgment or disapproval can keep you from taking action or standing up for what you truly want.

Perhaps the most painful area where guilt and shame impact adult children of narcissists is in **relationships**. When you grow up being told that you're unworthy or flawed, it's hard to believe that anyone could truly love you for who you are. You may find it difficult to trust others, fearing that they'll eventually see your "flaws" and abandon you. This fear can lead to toxic relationships where you either become overly compliant, trying to earn love and validation, or distant and avoidant, protecting yourself from getting hurt. The cycle of seeking approval, feeling unworthy, and doubting yourself can repeat itself in relationships, leading to loneliness, isolation, and confusion.

The Psychological Toll of Guilt and Shame

The psychological impact of guilt and shame isn't just emotional—it can also affect **mental health**. Research shows that chronic feelings of shame and guilt are linked to anxiety, depression, and low self-worth. When a child is taught to internalize the belief that they are the problem, it creates a vicious cycle of self-blame and emotional dysregulation. This emotional imbalance can manifest as overwhelming stress, feeling "on edge" all the time, or struggling with intrusive thoughts and negative self-talk.

When guilt and shame are left unaddressed, they can lead to a sense of **unworthiness** that colors every aspect of life. You might feel like you're never deserving of love, success, or happiness, and you may even push people away to avoid getting hurt. This sense of unworthiness is deeply ingrained and often keeps people in a place of emotional stagnation, where they feel like they can't move forward, no matter how much they want to.

Reflective Questions to Uncover the Roots of Guilt and Shame

It's crucial to recognize that these feelings are not your fault. They are the result of a toxic upbringing, not a reflection of who you truly are. To help you begin the process of untangling these emotions, take a moment to reflect on the following questions:

1. **When did you first start feeling like you were never enough?**

____

____

____

____

____

____

____

____

Was there a specific event or pattern in your childhood that made you feel this way?

____

____

____

2. **How do you talk to yourself when you make a mistake?**

____

____

____

____

____

____

____

Are you overly critical or forgiving? How does your inner voice compare to the way you would treat a loved one who made a mistake?

____

____

____

3. **What does "being good enough" look like to you?**

____

____

____

____

____

____

____

Is it based on external validation, or can you define it for yourself?

____

____

____

4. **How do you respond to compliments or praise from others?**

____

____

____

____

____

____

Do you accept them graciously, or do you dismiss them because you feel undeserving?

____

____

____

____

5. What would it take for you to believe that you are worthy of love and happiness?

____

____

____

____

____

____

____

Is there a shift you need to make in how you see yourself?

____

____

____

____

Gaslighting 101

Gaslighting is a term that gets tossed around a lot these days, but if you've grown up with a narcissistic parent, it's more than just a buzzword—it's likely been a major force in shaping your world. It's a form of psychological manipulation that's subtle but powerful. Imagine this: you have a memory or a feeling, but someone you trust, someone you look up to—your parent—tells you that what you remember or feel isn't true. That they never said that, or that you're overreacting. Over time, you start to doubt your own mind. Sound familiar? That's gaslighting at work.

Let's break it down.

What Gaslighting Looks Like in Narcissistic Parenting

Gaslighting isn't always a grand gesture. In fact, it's often the little things that chip away at your confidence and sense of reality. Narcissistic parents use gaslighting to keep their children under control, ensuring they stay dependent, obedient, and unaware of their own power. When your parent denies something you clearly remember, or twists the truth to make you second-guess your own experiences, that's gaslighting.

For example:

- **"I never said that. You're just imagining things."** You know they said it, but when they deny it so convincingly, you start to wonder if your memory is faulty.

- **"You're too sensitive, I was just joking."** If your parent makes a cutting comment or behaves in a way that hurts you, but then shrugs it off as if you're the problem, they're minimizing your feelings, making you question if you're overreacting.

- **"I don't remember that happening, you must be making things up."** If your parent flat-out denies your experiences, it creates confusion. What you remember clearly becomes something you're supposed to doubt.

These examples show how narcissistic parents manipulate their children's reality by creating confusion and planting seeds of self-doubt. They shift blame onto the child, making them feel responsible for the confusion they're experiencing.

The Emotional and Mental Toll of Gaslighting

Living with constant gaslighting takes a heavy toll on your mental and emotional well-being. At first, you might feel like you're just being too sensitive, but over time, gaslighting can leave you questioning everything. Are you really the problem? Did that really happen the way you remember? It's as if someone's playing tricks on your mind, and it's exhausting. When a parent consistently twists your perceptions, it fosters deep confusion about your feelings, actions, and memories.

The impact of gaslighting is more than just frustrating—it chips away at your sense of self. You might start to feel like you can't trust your own thoughts or instincts. Your ability to accurately interpret events and gauge your emotional responses becomes cloudy. This leads to a fragile sense of reality, where you constantly seek validation from others, unsure if your feelings are justified. Over time, this can develop into an overwhelming sense of insecurity.

Why Gaslighting Is Particularly Harmful

What makes gaslighting so damaging is that it doesn't just distort your view of the world—it erodes your trust in yourself. When a narcissistic parent constantly invalidates your feelings or denies your experiences, you begin to feel like you're not allowed to feel what you feel, or that your memories are unreliable. In essence, you lose the ability to trust your own mind.

This can lead to a cycle of self-doubt, where you constantly seek reassurance from others, but still feel unsure about your own perceptions. This confusion can spill over into relationships outside the family, causing difficulty in trusting others or even in your own decision-making. You might second-guess yourself, not just about your past experiences, but about your choices, feelings, and even your worth.

When this self-doubt takes root, it creates a vulnerability that narcissistic parents can exploit, leaving you stuck in a toxic cycle where your reality is shaped by someone else. Your emotional and mental well-being are tethered to someone who has no interest in your truth—only their control.

Recognizing Gaslighting in Your Own Life

You might be reading this and wondering, "Was I gaslighted?" If so, the answer is probably yes, but recognizing it is the first step toward healing. To help you start identifying gaslighting in your life, here are a few reflective prompts:

1. **Think back to a recent conversation with a parent (or anyone who has gaslighted you). What happened?** Were you made to feel like your feelings were invalid? Were your memories questioned or dismissed?

2. **How often do you second-guess yourself after a disagreement?** Do you find yourself

apologizing for things you aren't sure you did wrong, just to keep the peace?

3. **Notice how you feel in interactions with people who have a history of invalidating you.** Are you anxious, confused, or unsure of your thoughts and emotions?

Exercise: Spend some time writing down moments where you've felt gaslighted—times when your perceptions were dismissed or your reality twisted. Notice the patterns in these situations. How do they make you feel? How have they shaped your interactions with others?

Rebuilding Trust in Yourself

Now that you've started to recognize the signs of gaslighting, it's time to work on rebuilding trust in your own perceptions and feelings. This takes time, but it's absolutely possible. One way to begin is by practicing self-validation—acknowledging your feelings as real and valid, even if others don't understand them.

Exercise: Every day, write down one thing you felt or experienced that day. Then, write a validating statement to yourself. For example: "I felt frustrated when my parent dismissed my feelings, and it's okay for me to feel that way."

Recognizing and acknowledging your own truth is one of the first steps in healing from gaslighting. You don't need anyone else to validate your experiences. Your feelings matter, and they are real.

Gaslighting leaves deep emotional scars, but with time and self-compassion, you can reclaim your sense of reality and your emotional strength. Healing from gaslighting means trusting yourself again—and that's the first step toward breaking free from the confusion and pain you've carried for so long.

Letting Yourself Grieve

Grief is a deeply personal journey, and when it comes to grieving the childhood you never had, the pain can feel all-encompassing. You may not have had the parents who showed up for you in the way you needed. You may have felt abandoned, neglected, or trapped in a cycle of emotional manipulation. And now, as an adult, you are left with the difficult reality that your childhood was missing something vital. There's a profound loss in realizing that the love, validation, and emotional safety that every child deserves were never fully present. And it hurts—sometimes in ways words can't easily explain. If this resonates with you, I want to start by saying: **It's okay to grieve.** In fact, grieving is not just normal, it's necessary for your healing.

The Importance of Grieving Your Lost Childhood

When you've grown up with a narcissistic parent, your needs—emotional, physical, and psychological—were often secondary, if not entirely ignored. Instead of being seen, validated, and loved for who you are, you may have been expected to serve the emotional needs of the narcissistic parent. This leaves a deep wound, one that may feel like a hollow space inside you—like something essential was taken away.

Grieving that lost childhood is not about dwelling in the past or wishing things had been different. It's about acknowledging the truth of what you experienced and giving yourself permission to mourn the loss of the nurturing, safe, and healthy childhood that should have been yours. Grieving allows you to process the emotional damage caused by your upbringing and start the healing process. It's important to remember that grief is not a sign of weakness—it's a sign of strength. It means you're honoring the reality of your experience, and you're allowing yourself to heal.

The Emotional Stages of Grief and How They Show Up

Grief doesn't have a clear, linear path. It's messy, unpredictable, and can take unexpected turns. And that's okay. You may feel stuck in one phase for a while, or you may bounce from one stage to another, often without warning. It's important to understand the emotional stages of grief and how they might show up for you as you process the loss of your childhood:

- **Denial**: This is often the first defense mechanism. You may find yourself minimizing your experiences, telling yourself that others had it worse, or pretending the emotional damage doesn't exist. You might even wonder if your feelings are "too much." But the truth is, your feelings are valid. This stage is just your mind's way of trying to protect you from overwhelming pain.

- **Anger**: It's natural to feel angry when you realize how deeply you were hurt. You might feel anger toward your narcissistic parent for what they didn't provide. You might feel anger toward yourself for not being able to "fix" the situation or for how long it took you to recognize the damage done. Anger is an important step in letting yourself feel what's been suppressed for so long.

- **Bargaining**: This stage might look like you trying to rewrite history in your mind, wishing you could have been better or done something different. You might find yourself wondering, "If only I had been more obedient, maybe things would have been different." But it's crucial to remind yourself that you did the best you could with what you had, and the blame lies squarely with the dysfunctional dynamics you were subjected to, not with your worth or efforts.

- **Depression**: As you begin to fully confront the reality of what was lost, you may feel a wave of sadness or even despair. This is where the heaviness can feel almost unbearable—when you realize how deeply the emotional neglect has impacted you. This phase is a natural and necessary part of grieving. It's how your body processes the pain and sorrow you've been holding onto.

- **Acceptance**: Acceptance doesn't mean you're "over" your past. It means you've come to terms with it. You understand the role your upbringing has played in shaping who you are, but you no longer let it control or define you. You've begun to heal, and while the past is still a part of your story, it no longer holds power over your future.

Processing and Expressing Your Emotions

It's vital to give yourself the space to process these emotions rather than suppress them. Acknowledging your grief is one of the most powerful things you can do to move forward. Here are some ways you can begin to process and express these deep emotions:

- **Journaling**: Writing can be incredibly cathartic. Try writing letters to your younger self, or journal about how the grief of losing the childhood you deserved feels in the present. You might write about what you wish you had heard as a child or what you feel was unfairly taken from you. Don't worry about structure—just let the emotions flow.

- **Therapy**: Working with a therapist can provide a safe, supportive space for you to express and process these emotions. A professional can help guide you through the grief stages and give you the tools to navigate your feelings in a healthy way.

- **Creative Outlets**: Art, music, or movement can also help you express emotions that words alone can't capture. If you find it hard to talk about your pain, try putting it into something physical, like painting, dancing, or even gardening.

It's Okay to Feel

You might feel like it's too much to carry, or that your grief somehow makes you weak. But I want to remind you: it's okay to feel sad, angry, or hurt about what you missed out on. These emotions don't make you fragile; they make you human. Grieving is not a sign of being broken. It's a sign of being brave enough to face the truth and start the healing process.

Reflective Exercise:

Take a moment and ask yourself:

1. *What did I miss out on as a child?*

____

____

____

____

____

____

____

____

2. **What do I wish my parent had been able to give me emotionally?**

____

____

____

____

____

____

3. **How do I feel now about those unmet needs?**

____

____

____

____

____

____

____

____

Allow yourself to feel whatever comes up—there is no wrong answer. The important thing is that you're starting to acknowledge the grief and take the first steps toward healing. This process is not easy, but it's worth it. You deserve to feel your pain, honor your loss, and ultimately, find peace.

Chapter 3

How It Messed with Your Mind

Have you ever felt like you're carrying a weight you can't quite explain? A heaviness in your chest, a constant hum of anxiety, or a deep-seated sense that something is wrong with you, even though you've done nothing to deserve it? If you're nodding, you're not alone. Many adult children of narcissistic parents grapple with the emotional aftermath of their upbringing. It's like living with a shadow, one that shapes how you see yourself, interact with others, and navigate life's challenges. But what exactly is that weight? And why does it feel like it's never truly gone, no matter how hard you try to move forward?

The emotional landscape shaped by narcissistic parents is often a tangled mess of guilt, shame, and self-doubt. It's not just about feeling like you're never good enough—though that's a big part of it—it's about feeling like you *don't* know who you are at all. Growing up in an environment where love was conditional, based on how well you could meet your parent's needs or boost their ego, leaves deep emotional scars that aren't always easy to identify. You're left with feelings of inadequacy, confusion about your worth, and an overwhelming sense of emotional chaos. This chapter will help you make sense of those feelings and give you a foundation for understanding why your emotions have always been so complicated.

First, let's dive into the emotions that you might carry with you: **guilt** and **shame**. You probably know them well—those little voices in your head that tell you, "It's your fault things went wrong," or, "You're not enough." These are the lingering effects of emotional manipulation, gaslighting, and the unhealthy dynamics that can thrive in a narcissistic household. Narcissistic parents often condition their children to feel responsible for their behavior, making you believe that their anger, neglect, or lack of affection is somehow your fault. It's not. But it's so deeply ingrained in you that it can feel like truth. The shame, too, can be overwhelming. When a parent constantly criticizes or undermines you, it's easy to internalize those messages. "I'm not lovable," "I'm unworthy," "I'm a disappointment" become beliefs you carry into adulthood. But here's the truth: none of these beliefs are yours—they were handed to you by someone who should have been a source of love and validation.

Then there's **gaslighting**—a form of manipulation that makes you doubt your own perceptions of reality. Growing up with a narcissistic parent often means your feelings and experiences are dismissed or outright invalidated. Your emotions are belittled, or even worse, you're made to believe that what you saw, heard, or felt never happened at all. Over time, you start questioning your own sanity, feeling like you're trapped in a world where the truth is always shifting.

All of this leads to a **grief** that you may have never fully acknowledged—the grief of the childhood you never had. It's the grief of never feeling fully seen or loved for who you were, of always trying to prove yourself and failing. This loss isn't just about missing out on affection, it's about the emotional support, guidance, and safety that every child deserves but rarely receives in a narcissistic home. Allowing yourself to feel that grief can be incredibly healing—it's the first step in letting go of the emotional weight that's been holding you down.

By the end of this chapter, we'll take a closer look at how these emotional struggles aren't just random—they're deeply connected to the way you were raised. Understanding this is key to your healing journey. It's not your fault that you feel this way, but it is your responsibility to work through it and reclaim your life. The emotional scars from narcissistic parenting are deep, but they can heal. This chapter isn't just about naming the pain—it's about giving you the clarity and compassion you need to begin the healing process.

As we explore these feelings of guilt, shame, and grief, remember that they don't define you. They are part of your story, but they don't get to write your future. Together, we'll learn to untangle these emotions and reclaim the peace you deserve. You're already on the path to healing—just by acknowledging that these feelings exist, and that they don't have to control you anymore.

Who Am I Really?

For many adult children of narcissists, this experience is all too familiar. Narcissistic parents have a way of diminishing their children's identities—often without intending to, but with a devastating impact nonetheless. They do it through constant criticism, impossible standards, and an absence of genuine emotional support. Over time, this can cause a deep erosion of a child's self-esteem, leaving them uncertain of who they really are and struggling to trust their own thoughts and feelings.

Undermining Identity Through Criticism and Unrealistic Expectations

Growing up with a narcissistic parent means growing up with someone who sees you not as an individual, but as an extension of themselves. This often manifests in constant criticism. No matter how hard you try or how much effort you put into something, your best will never feel good enough. A narcissistic parent tends to set the bar unrealistically high, with expectations that are more about fulfilling their own needs than recognizing your abilities and potential.

If you've lived this way, you know how it feels: the sense that you're always falling short. Perhaps you were praised only when you met their standards, and even then, it was more about their own pride than your accomplishments. When they criticized, it wasn't constructive—more like a sharp reminder that you were, at best, "okay" but could always do better. This can be confusing. How do you trust your own judgment when the feedback you receive is never about who you are, but always about who you should be?

On top of the constant criticism, there's often a profound lack of emotional support. A narcissistic parent may be incapable of offering genuine warmth or encouragement because they are more focused on their own needs and image than on nurturing your emotional world. As a child, you may have longed for your parent's approval, but the love was conditional—if you didn't meet their expectations or fulfill their desires, you were met with indifference, or worse, punishment. This kind of emotional neglect leaves children feeling invisible, as if their needs don't matter. Over time, this fosters a deep sense of inadequacy, making it difficult to develop a clear understanding of who you are beyond the roles assigned to you by others.

The Impact on Self-Esteem and Self-Worth

When you're raised by a narcissistic parent, your sense of self-worth is often tied to external validation. This constant need for approval and affirmation makes it hard to develop a healthy internal sense of self. As an adult, you may find yourself still seeking validation from others—whether it's from romantic partners, friends, or coworkers. You might feel a nagging sense that you're never quite "enough" because, as a child, your worth was always measured by how you made your parent feel or how closely you adhered to their standards.

The effect on your self-esteem is deep and lasting. Narcissistic parents rarely allow their children to develop a sense of self that isn't based on their approval or disapproval. This can lead to feelings of inadequacy and confusion. You might constantly question your own decisions or feel like an imposter in your achievements, wondering if you've truly earned success or if it's all just luck or the result of external approval. When your parent's love felt conditional, it created a hole in your sense of self—a hole you may still struggle to fill as an adult.

Struggling with Self-Identity in Adulthood

As an adult child of a narcissist, the struggle for self-identity doesn't end when you leave home. In fact, it often becomes more pronounced as you try to build your life and relationships outside of the shadow of narcissistic influence. You might find it difficult to make decisions independently or trust your own instincts because, growing up, your voice was often silenced or ignored. Your thoughts and feelings were dismissed in favor of your parent's needs and desires. How can you possibly know who you are when, for years, you were expected to be someone else?

This uncertainty about your identity may lead to a cycle of seeking external validation. You might look for approval in your relationships, career, or social life, always measuring your worth against others' opinions. It can feel like you're constantly chasing an ideal self—a self that might be more reflective of others' expectations than your own. The fear of rejection or failure might lead to perfectionism, people-pleasing, or overachievement, all in an attempt to fill the void left by a lack of validation in your early years.

But this pursuit of approval often leaves you feeling empty, as if you're constantly reaching for something that's just out of your grasp. You may feel lost or confused about what truly makes you happy or fulfilled. The truth is, when your identity has been shaped by someone else's needs for so long, it's incredibly difficult to figure out who you are on your own terms.

Reflecting on Your Own Journey

Take a moment to reflect on your own experiences. How has your sense of self been shaped by your upbringing? Do you find yourself seeking approval from others, or questioning your worth when you're not praised or recognized? How do you react when your decisions or feelings are challenged? Are you comfortable trusting your instincts, or do you often second-guess yourself?

Here are some questions to help you explore your own self-identity:

1. ***What messages did you receive growing up about who you were?***

____

____

____

____

____

____

____

Did your parents celebrate your individuality, or were you expected to fit a specific mold?

____

____

____

____

2. *How does your inner dialogue sound today?*

Are you critical of yourself in the same way your parent was? What would it feel like to be kinder to yourself?

3. When was the last time you felt proud of something you did just for you?

____

____

____

____

____

____

____

____

Not for anyone else's approval, but because it felt right to you.

____

____

____

____

4. **What makes you feel "seen" or validated today?**

____

____

____

____

____

____

____

____

Do you find it difficult to feel confident without someone else's approval?

____

____

____

____

By reflecting on these questions, you can begin to untangle the layers of doubt and confusion that have built up over the years. Understanding how your upbringing affected your sense of self is the first step toward reclaiming your identity and embracing who you truly are, without the weight of past criticism or the need for external validation.

Why Relationships Feel Hard

For many adult children of narcissists, forming and maintaining healthy relationships can feel like navigating through a maze. The emotional scars left by narcissistic parenting can make it hard to trust, be vulnerable, and truly feel loved. And what's more frustrating is that you might not even fully understand why relationships feel so difficult, or why you keep repeating unhealthy patterns.

First, let's dive into something called **attachment theory**. Attachment theory is a psychological framework that explains how we form emotional bonds and connect with others, especially in childhood. The way your parents or primary caregivers responded to your needs shapes the way you'll relate to others in adulthood. This attachment system plays a huge role in your relationships throughout life—whether it's romantic, with friends, or even with colleagues.

Now, when you grow up with a narcissistic parent, the way you attach to others can be deeply affected. Narcissistic parents are often inconsistent, emotionally unavailable, and focused on their own needs, which leaves their children feeling unsupported or unloved. As a result, children of narcissists can develop **insecure attachment styles**, such as anxious or avoidant behaviors. These attachment styles can follow you into adulthood, making relationships feel like an emotional rollercoaster.

- **Anxious Attachment**: If you had a narcissistic parent, you might find yourself constantly seeking reassurance and fearing abandonment. You may feel like you're never good enough and worry that people will leave you. You might overthink small things your partner says or does, wondering if you're doing something wrong. You may also become overly clingy or dependent, as your emotional needs were often unmet in the past.

- **Avoidant Attachment**: On the other hand, some adult children of narcissists develop an avoidant attachment style. This can look like shutting down emotionally, pushing people away, or fearing vulnerability. You may struggle to open up to others or find it hard to connect with your partner on a deep level. There's a fear of getting too close because you've learned to protect yourself from getting hurt.

Both attachment styles—whether anxious or avoidant—stem from an early childhood where love was conditional, unpredictable, or absent. The result? Difficulty in trusting others and building stable, emotionally fulfilling relationships as adults.

Emotional Walls and Defense Mechanisms

Many adult children of narcissists also build **emotional walls** to protect themselves. After all, if your parent was emotionally unavailable or critical, you learned that showing vulnerability could lead to rejection or hurt. Over time, you may have found ways to block out your feelings to keep from being hurt again. These emotional walls are like an armor that makes it harder to let people in.

As a result, you might develop **defense mechanisms** to cope with difficult emotions or the fear of being hurt. Some common defenses include:

- **People-pleasing**: You might constantly try to keep others happy, afraid of conflict or rejection.

This behavior often comes from a deep fear of being abandoned, as your needs were often ignored or dismissed in childhood.

- **Perfectionism**: Trying to be perfect might be your way of seeking approval or trying to control a situation to avoid criticism. In childhood, you may have been held to impossible standards by your narcissistic parent, and now you feel that if you don't get everything right, you'll be rejected.

- **Emotional numbness**: In an effort to protect yourself from the overwhelming emotions that come with deep connection, you might find yourself shutting off your feelings altogether. This numbness can leave you feeling distant, even in relationships where you want to be close.

These defenses are your brain's way of coping with past trauma, but they often create barriers to forming real, trusting connections with others. They may give you a sense of safety in the short term, but in the long run, they can prevent you from having the deep, meaningful relationships you deserve.

The Struggles of Trust, Intimacy, and Emotional Connection

When you've been raised in an environment where emotional needs were neglected or invalidated, it's no surprise that trust becomes a significant issue. **Fear of intimacy** often arises because being emotionally vulnerable can feel risky or even dangerous. Letting someone see your true self can stir up deep fears of rejection or betrayal, fears that were likely developed from your experiences with your narcissistic parent.

Moreover, **difficulty trusting** others can be one of the hardest hurdles to overcome. If your parent made you feel like you could never rely on them, it's understandable that you'd carry that mistrust into other relationships. You might question the motives of others or constantly wonder if someone is going to hurt you, even when they've shown no signs of doing so. This mistrust can create friction and insecurity in relationships, making it hard for you to experience true intimacy.

Another common issue is the tendency to either **over-invest** in relationships or **withdraw** completely. If you've experienced rejection or emotional neglect, you may either overcompensate by putting too much effort into pleasing others or become emotionally distant to protect yourself from future hurt. These extremes can cause strain in relationships and make it difficult for you to find balance.

Strategies for Healing and Building Healthier Relationships

So, what can you do to start healing these attachment wounds and building healthier relationships?

1. **Recognize Your Attachment Style**: The first step is awareness. By understanding your attachment style (whether anxious, avoidant, or somewhere in between), you can begin to identify the patterns that have been holding you back in relationships. Pay attention to your reactions in relationships—do you become overly clingy, or do you shut down emotionally?

2. **Start Practicing Vulnerability**: It's going to feel uncomfortable at first, but opening up to trusted people is one of the best ways to begin healing. Vulnerability is the antidote to emotional walls. Start small—share a fear, a hope, or a personal dream with someone you trust. Gradually, you'll build the muscles of intimacy.

3. **Challenge Negative Beliefs About Yourself**: Many adult children of narcissists struggle with low self-esteem. Remind yourself that you are worthy of love and respect, just as you are. Practice self-compassion and confront the negative self-talk that tells you you're not enough.

4. **Set Healthy Boundaries**: If your relationships are marked by people-pleasing or emotional enmeshment, learning to set boundaries is key. Boundaries are not about shutting people out; they are about respecting your needs and creating space for healthy interactions.

5. **Seek Therapy or Support**: Healing from narcissistic abuse often requires outside help. Therapy can provide a safe space to unpack your feelings, address unresolved trauma, and develop healthier relational patterns. Support groups or trusted friends can also help you feel less alone in your journey.

Relationships may feel hard, but with understanding, self-awareness, and healing, you can build the trust and connection that once seemed impossible. It's not about perfection—it's about progress and giving yourself permission to grow. You deserve deep, fulfilling relationships, and with time and effort, you can make that a reality.

Coping Mechanisms You Didn't Sign Up For

Growing up with a narcissistic parent isn't just challenging in the moment—it shapes how you view yourself and interact with the world long after you've left home. One of the most common yet unseen ways this happens is through the coping mechanisms you develop.

These behaviors, often formed in childhood as survival strategies, can feel like second nature. But here's the catch: You didn't consciously choose them. They weren't decisions made with your best interests in mind. Instead, they were ways to navigate an environment that was emotionally unpredictable, where your needs were often overlooked or even invalidated.

How These Coping Mechanisms Develop

As a child, your primary job is to feel safe, loved, and accepted. But when your parent is narcissistic, these needs often go unmet. Narcissistic parents can be demanding, emotionally distant, or excessively critical. As a result, you may have developed certain patterns of behavior to survive—ones that, while they helped you manage the chaos at the time, don't always serve you as an adult.

These behaviors become ingrained over time. Whether you're consciously aware of them or not, they show up in your relationships, your career, and your personal sense of self-worth. It's important to understand that these coping mechanisms were never your fault. You were simply trying to get through life in the best way you knew how, given the circumstances. But the truth is, these mechanisms, while protective, are often unhealthy and can lead to ongoing struggles like burnout, emotional overwhelm, and chronic dissatisfaction.

Common Coping Mechanisms and Their Impact

Let's explore three of the most common coping mechanisms that children of narcissists tend to develop: **people-pleasing**, **perfectionism**, and **conflict avoidance**. These behaviors often feel like the only way to survive in a world that doesn't offer unconditional support.

1. People-Pleasing

People-pleasing is perhaps the most insidious of the coping strategies because it can look so socially acceptable on the surface. As a child of a narcissist, you may have learned early on that in order to receive love, attention, or even basic emotional validation, you had to please those around you. Maybe it was doing whatever it took to make your parent happy, even if it meant sacrificing your own desires or well-being.

As an adult, this can translate into always saying "yes" to others, even when you feel overwhelmed or resentful. You might take on more responsibilities than you can handle, constantly seeking approval or avoiding conflict at all costs. On the outside, people may see you as accommodating or generous, but inside, you're often running on empty.

Downside: The emotional cost of people-pleasing is high. You may feel exhausted, unappreciated, or even resentful when your needs are ignored. Over time, it can lead to burnout, anxiety, and feelings of being invisible or undervalued.

Scenario: You're asked to take on a project at work, even though your plate is already full. Without hesitation, you agree because you don't want to disappoint anyone. Later, you feel frustrated because you're stretched too thin, but you're too afraid to speak up about it, fearing judgment or rejection.

2. Perfectionism

Perfectionism often arises as a defense against the constant criticism that comes with narcissistic parenting. In an environment where nothing is ever good enough, striving for perfection might have seemed like the only way to earn praise or avoid disapproval. This need to be flawless can stick with you well into adulthood.

As a perfectionist, you might set unrealistic expectations for yourself, believing that anything less than perfect will result in failure or criticism. You may spend excessive time on tasks, constantly double-checking your work, and overthinking every decision, because the idea of making a mistake feels terrifying.

Downside: While perfectionism might seem like a way to gain control or validation, it often backfires. It can lead to chronic dissatisfaction, as you're never able to meet your own impossibly high standards. It also prevents you from enjoying life or taking risks because the fear of failure is paralyzing.

Scenario: You spend hours preparing a report for work, obsessing over every detail. When it's finally submitted, it's perfectly done—but you still feel like it's not good enough. You criticize yourself for small things no one else would notice, and your stress levels skyrocket.

3. Conflict Avoidance

In a home where emotions were unpredictable or explosive, conflict avoidance became a survival mechanism. You may have learned that the best way to keep the peace was to stay quiet, keep your feelings to yourself, or simply comply with whatever your narcissistic parent wanted.

As an adult, this can show up as a deep fear of confrontation. You might go out of your way to avoid disagreements, even if it means suppressing your own needs or feelings. The thought of conflict may trigger intense anxiety, making it hard for you to assert yourself in relationships or at work.

Downside: Avoiding conflict may temporarily keep things calm, but it prevents you from addressing real issues. Over time, this can lead to pent-up frustration, unresolved resentment, and even passive-aggressive behaviors. You might also feel like you're walking on eggshells, constantly trying to avoid triggering someone else's emotions.

Scenario: Your partner asks you about plans for the weekend, but you're too tired to go out. Instead of saying you need a rest, you agree to go, knowing you'll be exhausted afterward. Later, you're frustrated with yourself for not speaking up, but you're afraid of rocking the boat.

Reflective Exercise
Recognizing Your Own Coping Mechanisms

1. Look at your behavior patterns:

Take a moment to reflect on how you typically respond in stressful situations. Are you quick to please others, even when it means neglecting your own needs? Do you set yourself up for perfection, only to feel disappointed with the results? Do you avoid confrontation at all costs, even if it means suppressing your true feelings?

2. Name your coping strategies:

Write down the coping strategies that seem to show up most often in your life. People-pleasing? Perfectionism? Conflict avoidance? Others? Be honest with yourself and give each behavior a name. Understanding what they are is the first step toward changing them.

3. Challenge these behaviors:

Ask yourself: How do these behaviors make me feel in the long run? Do they help me build meaningful connections or just leave me feeling drained and resentful? Take note of any patterns and think about healthier ways to cope with stress or emotional triggers. For example, what would it look like to speak up in a situation where you usually avoid conflict? How might you set a boundary instead of overextending yourself?

Healing isn't about eliminating these coping mechanisms overnight; it's about recognizing them and learning to choose healthier alternatives. As you become aware of how these strategies show up in your life, you can begin to consciously choose new ways of handling stress, relationships, and your own emotions.

By acknowledging these survival strategies, you take the first step in freeing yourself from their grip. With time, self-compassion, and practice, you can move toward healthier, more balanced ways of coping. The goal is not perfection, but progress—learning to live in a way that honors your true self and supports your well-being.

List three ways your upbringing shaped your view of yourself and relationships. Are they still true for you today?

____

____

____

____

____

____

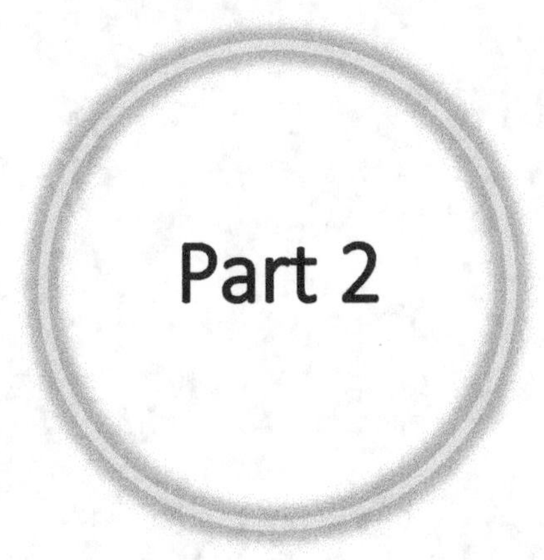

BREAKING FREE FROM OLD PATTERNS

Taking Back Your Power, One Step at a Time

Chapter 4

Spotting the Patterns Holding You Back

For many adult children of narcissists, this is a common experience. You may not even realize that the roots of your self-doubt, your fear of making mistakes, or your need for constant approval were planted in childhood, shaped by the behaviors and expectations of your narcissistic parent. These subtle, almost invisible patterns were absorbed over years, deeply influencing the way you see yourself and how you react in everyday situations. It's not your fault, but recognizing these patterns is the first step in breaking free.

This chapter is all about helping you uncover those patterns. As you read on, you'll gain insight into how your upbringing has quietly dictated so many of your choices and reactions as an adult. Narcissistic parents often have a way of making their children feel responsible for their emotions, demanding perfection, or manipulating them into believing that their worth depends on how much they give. These behaviors might not have been glaringly obvious when you were a child, but they shaped your emotional responses and decision-making processes in profound ways.

Understanding these patterns isn't just important for your emotional clarity—it's essential for your healing. The more you recognize how the past is affecting your present, the more power you have to change it. This chapter will provide you with practical tools to help you identify your emotional triggers, understand why certain situations leave you feeling small or helpless, and learn how to break out of the patterns that have held you back for so long.

I know this might feel overwhelming. Recognizing the ways in which you've been shaped by your narcissistic parent can bring up some difficult emotions—guilt, anger, or even sadness. But know this: You are not alone in this. It's completely normal for this process to feel uncomfortable at first, but it is also incredibly freeing. By uncovering these patterns, you are taking the first and most crucial step toward healing and creating a life that's authentically yours.

This chapter will guide you gently through the process of recognizing and understanding the toxic patterns that have shaped your life. With each page, you'll be uncovering more of your truth, and with that truth, comes the power to heal. You've already taken a courageous step by picking up this book—now, let's take the next step together, one pattern at a time.

Why You Do What You Do

You might recognize this feeling: You're at work, and your boss asks you to take on a task that's outside your usual responsibilities. It's something that feels overwhelming, and deep down, you're unsure if you can handle it. But instead of voicing your concerns, you immediately agree, trying to appear confident and capable. Inside, you're anxious, worried about failing, and wondering if you're good enough. Yet, outwardly, you push those thoughts aside and take on the challenge, hoping to earn validation or approval. It's a pattern many adult children of narcissistic parents know well. Whether it's in work, relationships, or daily life, the tendency to please others and avoid any form of conflict can be deeply ingrained.

For many of us, this pattern began in childhood. Growing up in a narcissistic household, approval was often a rare commodity—something you had to earn, sometimes at great personal cost. The idea of being accepted or loved was tied to meeting someone else's needs, often at the expense of your own. This meant suppressing your true self, changing your behavior to match what your parent wanted, and constantly worrying about their reaction. Over time, these survival mechanisms—people-pleasing, perfectionism, and the fear of conflict—became second nature, carrying you through a childhood full of emotional minefields. Unfortunately, these patterns, while they once helped you navigate a volatile environment, can now hold you back from fully living your life as an adult.

As a child of a narcissist, you were likely raised in an environment where love and attention were conditional. Your worth was determined by how well you could meet your parent's needs, fulfill their expectations, and avoid triggering their anger or disappointment. You quickly learned that approval and love were scarce, and it was up to you to make sure you earned it. Unfortunately, this meant learning to shrink yourself, to mold your identity around what your parent wanted you to be, in order to be seen and accepted. The constant fear of rejection, the pressure to be perfect, and the need to maintain peace at all costs became part of your survival toolkit.

But here's the tricky part: these habits, which once helped you navigate the storm of narcissistic parenting, are now holding you back from fully living your life as an adult. You might find yourself stuck in a loop—saying yes to things you don't want to do, avoiding conflict even when it hurts you, or constantly striving for perfection in a world where nothing is ever "good enough." These ingrained behaviors no longer serve you in a healthy way, and they can keep you from stepping into the fullness of who you are meant to be.

Let's explore some of these behaviors in more detail.

People-Pleasing: The Never-Ending Struggle for Approval

As a child, you may have learned that the only way to get your parent's attention, affection, or even approval was to please them. This meant suppressing your own needs and desires to cater to theirs. If you did something wrong, you were likely met with criticism, so you quickly learned to avoid rocking the boat. In adulthood, this often shows up as a constant need to please others, even at your own expense. You might overcommit at work, say yes to every request from family or friends, and feel guilty when you can't be everything to everyone.

But here's the truth: people-pleasing doesn't actually get you the validation you're seeking. It keeps you stuck in a cycle of seeking external approval because you never learned to validate yourself. Over time, this leaves you feeling drained, resentful, and disconnected from your own needs.

Fear of Conflict: The Perfection of Avoidance

In a narcissistic household, conflict was dangerous. Your narcissistic parent may have escalated minor disagreements into explosive arguments or punished you for standing up for yourself. The fear of conflict becomes a learned behavior, something you carry with you into adulthood. Even if you're dealing with a healthy, respectful partner or friend, the fear of confrontation can paralyze you, making you avoid necessary discussions or brush things under the rug. You might suppress your own opinions or avoid confronting people when something isn't right—because deep down, you're terrified of the fallout.

The problem with this is that avoiding conflict doesn't resolve anything—it only lets issues fester beneath the surface. The inability to express your thoughts or feelings can leave you feeling unheard, unseen, and ultimately dissatisfied in your relationships.

Perfectionism: The Need to Be "Perfect" to Be Loved

Perfectionism often goes hand-in-hand with narcissistic parenting. Growing up, you might have been told that you weren't good enough unless you achieved at a certain level—whether in grades, appearance, behavior, or other ways. This created an underlying belief that love and approval were only possible if you were perfect, or at least appeared perfect on the outside. As an adult, this might show up as an obsessive need to do everything flawlessly, constantly second-guessing yourself, and pushing yourself beyond reasonable limits.

The problem with perfectionism is that it's an impossible standard to live up to. No one can be perfect all the time, and yet, you keep striving for that unattainable goal, leaving you exhausted, frustrated, and constantly feeling like you're falling short.

The Need for Validation: A Never-Filling Void

From a young age, you were conditioned to seek validation from others. Whether it was your parent's approval, praise for your accomplishments, or acknowledgment for being "good," your sense of self-worth became entangled with how others perceived you.

This can make it incredibly difficult to feel secure in who you are, without constant reassurance from others. In adulthood, the desire for validation might show up in unhealthy relationships, staying in jobs where you feel unappreciated, or constantly trying to win approval from those around you.

But true validation comes from within. When you are constantly seeking external affirmation, you are giving away your power to others. Learning to validate yourself, independent of external sources, is key to breaking free from this pattern.

Reflective Questions to Help You Dig Deeper:

1. Do you find yourself agreeing to things you don't want to do just to keep the peace? How does that make you feel afterward?

____

____

____

____

____

____

2. What's your typical response when there's a disagreement? Do you avoid it, sweep it under the rug, or confront it head-on?

____

____

____

____

3. What are the areas in your life where you feel you must be perfect? How does this affect your peace of mind and relationships?

____

____

____

____

____

4. How often do you seek approval from others? What would it look like for you to validate yourself, regardless of outside opinions?

____

____

____

____

____

____

By reflecting on these questions, you'll begin to recognize where these ingrained habits and beliefs stem from. The goal is not to shame yourself for having them—these behaviors kept you safe as a child, but they no longer serve you in adulthood. By understanding where they come from, you can begin the process of untangling these old patterns and making room for healthier, more authentic ways of living.

The journey ahead may not always be easy, but recognizing why you do what you do is the first step toward freeing yourself from the past and building a future that's all about *you*—not the version of yourself shaped by someone else's needs.

Trigger Troubles

You're sitting at work, trying to get through a normal day. It's been a busy morning, but things are starting to settle down. Then, you get an email from your boss. At first glance, it seems like a simple request for an update on a project, nothing out of the ordinary. But something about the tone rubs you the wrong way. It feels critical, as if you're being subtly judged or scolded, even though the words themselves are mild. Suddenly, your heart starts racing, your hands feel clammy, and before you know it, you're overwhelmed by emotions that seem to come out of nowhere. In that moment, you realize it's not just about the email—it's a trigger. That feeling, that gut reaction, is bringing you back to a past place, where old wounds resurface, even though you're trying to move on.

It's not just a simple email. It's a trigger. And before you know it, the floodgates open. You're hit with a wave of old emotions—shame, guilt, and inadequacy. You feel that familiar knot in your stomach, as though you've disappointed someone you can't quite please. The reaction doesn't seem to match the situation, but that's the nature of triggers. They pull you back into an emotional moment from your past, often one you don't fully understand.

What Are Emotional Triggers and Flashbacks?

An emotional trigger is a situation, word, or even a tone of voice that brings up strong emotions tied to past events—often ones you've been trying to move beyond. Flashbacks, on the other hand, are a more intense experience where you mentally and emotionally relive a past moment as though it's happening again, right now. This could be a memory of a parent belittling you or a moment of being ignored or dismissed.

For adult children of narcissists, these triggers can be particularly jarring because they're rooted in long-held, unresolved emotional wounds. Growing up with a narcissistic parent often means you were subjected to emotional manipulation, harsh criticism, and a constant sense of never being enough. Over time, these experiences become deeply ingrained in your psyche, and they don't just disappear when you leave home or grow older. Instead, they simmer beneath the surface, waiting for a moment to resurface.

Common Triggers for Adult Children of Narcissists

One of the most common triggers for adult children of narcissists is criticism—whether it's direct or implied. Growing up with a parent who constantly pointed out your flaws, you might have internalized a belief that you are never good enough. As an adult, any slight criticism—no matter how small—can trigger that deep-rooted feeling of inadequacy.

Rejection is another powerful trigger. As children, you may have been made to feel invisible or unworthy of love and attention unless you were meeting someone else's needs. This can make rejection—whether in relationships, work, or even friendships—feel like a personal attack. The emotional wound of being rejected can feel like being that child again, trying desperately to earn your parent's love but always falling short.

Then there's the experience of being ignored or neglected. Narcissistic parents often prioritize their own needs over their children's, leaving their children to feel invisible or unimportant. As an adult, you might find yourself hypersensitive to being overlooked in social situations or dismissed in conversations. The intensity of these feelings often seems disproportionate to the situation, but that's the nature of triggers—they bring you back to an old, unresolved emotional place.

How to Manage and Recognize Your Triggers

The first step in managing triggers is recognizing them. When you're caught off guard by a wave of emotions that seems out of proportion to what's happening in the present moment, pause. Take a deep breath and ask yourself, "Is this really about what's happening right now? Or is this reminding me of something from my past?"

Self-awareness is key to this process. By recognizing that your reaction is tied to past trauma, you begin to separate the present from the past. Understanding that your emotional flashbacks are not just random, but responses to old wounds, can help you gain a sense of control over them. It's like being able to recognize a storm cloud on the horizon before it hits—you see it coming and can prepare yourself.

Self-compassion is also critical in this process. It's easy to beat yourself up for "overreacting" when you're triggered, but that's not helpful. Instead, try offering yourself the same kindness you would offer a friend who was going through something similar. Tell yourself, "It's okay to feel this way. It's not your fault. You're healing, and this is part of the process." Be gentle with yourself, because healing from narcissistic abuse takes time, and triggers are a normal part of that journey.

Practical Strategies for Responding to Triggers

Once you recognize a trigger, the next step is to respond in a healthier way. Here are a few strategies that can help:

1. **Pause and Breathe:** When you feel a trigger rising, stop and take a few slow, deep breaths. This can help reset your nervous system and give you space to process your emotions. Sometimes, just breathing deeply can make a huge difference in how you handle a situation.

2. **Label the Emotion:** Put a name to what you're feeling—whether it's anger, fear, sadness, or something else. Acknowledging the emotion can help you distance yourself from it and regain some control.

3. **Challenge the Belief:** When you feel the old feelings of shame or inadequacy flood in, challenge those beliefs. Ask yourself, "Is this feeling based on who I am now? Or is it an echo of something my parent made me believe as a child?"

4. **Ground Yourself in the Present:** Remind yourself that you're no longer that child. Use grounding techniques like focusing on the present moment, touching something familiar (like a piece

of jewelry or a favorite object), or repeating a positive affirmation to reconnect with reality.

5. **Reach Out for Support:** If you're struggling to process a trigger, talk to someone who understands—whether that's a friend, therapist, or support group. Sharing what you're going through can provide relief and perspective.

Practical Exercise: Identifying Your Triggers

Take a moment to reflect on situations in the past few weeks that have triggered strong emotional reactions in you. Write down the specific events that caused these feelings. Then, ask yourself:

- What feelings did these situations stir up? (Shame, guilt, anger, fear?)

____

____

____

____

____

____

- Do these emotions remind you of a time in your childhood? If so, what happened then?

____

____

____

____

____

- How can you respond differently next time?

____

____

____

____

____

In your journal, write a plan for how you might handle these situations in the future. What steps can you take to detach from the emotional flashbacks and respond in a healthier way?

By becoming more aware of your triggers and developing coping strategies, you can break free from the automatic reactions that have been controlling you for so long. Healing doesn't happen overnight, but each small step you take makes a big difference.

Breaking Free from the Guilt Trap

Guilt can feel like an old, familiar shadow—always lingering, even when you're trying to move forward. It shows up in the quiet moments, tugging at your thoughts when you decide to prioritize yourself or say "no" to someone's request. For adult children of narcissists, this guilt is more than just a passing emotion; it's a deeply ingrained response, etched into the fabric of your life from years of walking on eggshells and putting others first.

This guilt didn't appear out of nowhere. Narcissistic parents often plant it intentionally, using it as a way to maintain control. They create an environment where their needs are always urgent, their feelings always fragile, and your role is to soothe, support, and sacrifice. Over time, you learn to equate love with obligation and care with self-denial, leaving little room for your own wants or needs.

Why Narcissists Use Guilt as a Weapon

Narcissistic parents often use guilt as a tool to maintain control and keep the focus on their needs. From a young age, you may have been conditioned to believe that their happiness, comfort, or approval depended entirely on your actions. If you didn't call when they expected, express gratitude "enough," or meet their unspoken demands, they made sure you felt the sting of disappointment or the weight of their hurt feelings.

This dynamic wasn't accidental—it was deliberate. Guilt is one of the easiest ways for a narcissist to manipulate others. It's subtle but powerful, ensuring you're always walking on eggshells, trying to do enough, be enough, or give enough. Over time, you internalize this behavior, and it morphs into a belief: **"If someone's upset, it must be my fault. It's my job to fix it."**

How Guilt Shows Up in Your Life

Even long after leaving the narcissist's orbit, the effects of this conditioning linger. Maybe you:

- Say "yes" to every request because saying "no" feels like betrayal.

- Constantly check and double-check that others are happy with you, fearing their disapproval.

- Feel responsible for solving problems that aren't yours to solve, from calming a friend's anxiety to picking up extra work to keep your boss happy.

- Put your own needs, desires, or boundaries on the back burner because prioritizing yourself feels selfish.

This guilt creates an exhausting cycle. The more you try to ease others' discomfort, the more you reinforce the belief that it's your responsibility. And the more you neglect your own needs, the more drained and resentful you feel—yet you still find yourself unable to stop.

Why Breaking the Cycle Matters

Living under the weight of guilt robs you of emotional freedom. It keeps you stuck in a pattern of people-pleasing and self-neglect, leaving little room for joy, authenticity, or true connection. The good news? You can break free. It won't happen overnight, but with time and intention, you can begin untangling yourself from guilt's grip.

Steps to Break Free from the Guilt Trap

1. Recognize That Guilt Is a Learned Response

Start by acknowledging that the guilt you feel isn't an accurate reflection of reality—it's a habit that developed in response to manipulation. Remind yourself: **Feeling guilty doesn't mean you've done something wrong.**

Reflective Exercise: Think of a recent situation where you felt guilty. Was it because you truly harmed someone, or because you didn't meet an unreasonable expectation? Write about how you would approach the same situation if guilt wasn't a factor.

2. Set Boundaries with Confidence

Boundaries are your antidote to guilt. They protect your energy, time, and well-being, allowing you to show up authentically in relationships without feeling trapped. Start small:

- Practice saying "no" without overexplaining.

- Limit how often you engage in guilt-triggering conversations.

- Use phrases like, "I hear you, but I can't take that on right now," to assert your limits kindly but firmly.

Case Study: Sarah, an adult child of a narcissistic father, shares how setting boundaries transformed her relationship dynamics—and how she handled the backlash with grace.

3. Challenge the Belief That You're Responsible for Others

A hard truth: You are not responsible for anyone else's happiness, emotions, or well-being. Remind yourself that everyone is in charge of their own feelings and choices, just as you are in charge of yours.

Journaling Prompt: Write down three situations where you felt responsible for someone's emotions. Ask yourself: "Was this truly my responsibility? Could they have managed this themselves?"

4. Practice Self-Compassion

Guilt thrives on self-criticism, so counter it with self-kindness. When guilt bubbles up, pause and ask: "If a friend felt this way, what would I tell them?" Treat yourself with the same care and understanding.

Daily Affirmation: "I deserve to prioritize my needs. Setting boundaries is not selfish—it's self-respect."

5. Celebrate Small Wins

Each time you resist guilt-driven behavior, you're rewriting years of conditioning. Celebrate your progress, no matter how small. Did you say "no" to a request? Take a moment to appreciate the courage it took. Did you prioritize your needs for once? That's a victory worth acknowledging.

Breaking free from guilt isn't about becoming unfeeling—it's about finding balance. It's about showing love and care to others without sacrificing your own well-being. Remember: You're allowed to take up space, prioritize your needs, and live without the constant weight of guilt. You've carried it long enough.

Chapter 5

Learning to Say "No" Without Guilt

It's a familiar scenario: You're exhausted from a long day, and a friend asks for a favor. Deep down, you know you don't have the time or energy, but instead of saying no, you hear yourself saying, "Sure, I can do that." As the call ends, frustration bubbles up inside—not at them, but at yourself. Why was it so hard to decline? If you've grown up with narcissistic parents, this moment might hit especially close to home. Saying "no" often feels impossible because you've been conditioned to believe your needs are less important than everyone else's.

For many adult children of narcissists, the idea of setting boundaries or prioritizing their own well-being feels wrong—almost selfish. That's no accident. Narcissistic parents often manipulate their children into compliance, using guilt, shame, or even affection as tools to maintain control. Over time, you might have internalized the belief that saying no makes you a bad person. But here's the truth: Saying no is not selfish; it's self-preservation.

This chapter is about taking back the power that was slowly stripped away. Learning to say no is one of the most liberating steps you can take toward reclaiming your autonomy. It's a way to protect your time, energy, and emotional health—things you might have sacrificed for too long. Saying no isn't just about declining requests; it's about valuing yourself enough to decide what you're willing to give.

We'll start by exploring why setting boundaries can feel so intimidating, especially for those of us who were taught that our worth is tied to how much we do for others. Then, we'll dive into practical steps to set boundaries that stick, from crafting clear responses to handling the guilt that often comes with standing your ground. Finally, we'll discuss how to navigate the pushback you might face from people who are used to you saying yes—because, let's be honest, not everyone will be thrilled when you start asserting yourself.

By the end of this chapter, you'll feel more confident in your ability to say no without guilt and, most importantly, without compromising the relationships that truly matter. It's time to put yourself first—not out of selfishness, but because you deserve it. Let's get started.

Why Boundaries Are Scary (But Necessary)

If the idea of setting boundaries makes your stomach churn, you're not alone. For adult children of narcissists, boundaries can feel like an impossible challenge—a minefield of potential rejection, anger, or punishment. Saying "no" might feel dangerous, as if asserting yourself could cost you the connection you've been trying so hard to preserve, no matter how unhealthy it might be.

Why is this so difficult? The answer lies in the dynamics of growing up with a narcissistic parent. Narcissistic parents often dismiss or punish their children's attempts to assert independence. They may frame your boundaries as a personal attack or accuse you of being selfish or ungrateful. Over time, you may have learned that expressing your needs or limits only leads to shame, guilt, or outright conflict.

But here's the truth: boundaries are not acts of rebellion; they're acts of self-preservation. They're the lines you draw to protect your emotional and mental health. Without them, you may find yourself drained, resentful, and disconnected from your own identity.

Why Boundaries Feel So Dangerous

Let's dig deeper into why boundaries are scary. For many adult children of narcissists, fear of rejection is at the heart of the issue. When your parent used love and approval as conditional rewards—dangling them just out of reach—you learned to suppress your own needs to keep the peace. The idea of setting a boundary might feel like risking the very connection you've been trained to value above all else.

There's also the fear of conflict. Narcissistic parents are masters of turning a simple "no" into a dramatic showdown. They might gaslight you ("You're imagining things"), guilt-trip you ("After everything I've done for you!"), or escalate the situation until you feel like it's just easier to give in. These experiences leave a lasting imprint, teaching you to avoid setting boundaries to escape the backlash.

Finally, there's the guilt. Narcissistic parents often convince their children that putting themselves first is inherently wrong. They paint self-care as selfishness and boundaries as betrayal. You may feel like asserting yourself makes you a bad person, even if logically you know that's not true.

The Role of Boundaries in Your Healing Journey

So, why bother with boundaries if they're so hard? Because they're essential to your healing. Boundaries are about reclaiming your right to exist as a separate, whole person. They're about protecting your energy, time, and emotional well-being.

Think of boundaries as the fence around a garden. Without a fence, anyone can trample your flowers, take what they want, or leave their mess behind. With a fence, you create a space where you can thrive. It's not about shutting people out entirely—it's about deciding who gets access to your time and energy and on what terms.

When you set boundaries, you stop living at the mercy of others' expectations. You start valuing your own needs and honoring your own limits. This shift isn't just liberating—it's life-changing.

What Happens Without Boundaries?

Without boundaries, you might find yourself constantly saying "yes" when you want to say "no." This can lead to burnout, as you pour your energy into everyone else's needs while neglecting your own. You may feel resentful toward others for taking advantage of you, but also angry at yourself for allowing it to happen. Over time, this dynamic erodes your sense of self, leaving you unsure of who you are or what you want.

Consider this example:

Imagine your narcissistic parent calling you at all hours, demanding your attention and expecting you to drop everything to meet their needs. Without boundaries, you might comply out of guilt or fear, even if it disrupts your work, sleep, or emotional balance. Over time, this pattern leaves you exhausted and feeling like your life isn't your own. With boundaries, however, you could set a limit—choosing specific times to engage or even explaining that you're unavailable during certain hours. It's not about rejecting the person; it's about protecting yourself.

Reflection Time: Your Fears and Your Needs

Take a moment to reflect on your own relationship with boundaries:

1. When you think about setting a boundary, what fears come up?

____

____

____

____

2. Are you afraid of being seen as selfish or ungrateful?

____

____

____

____

3. Can you identify past experiences where setting a boundary led to conflict or punishment?

____

____

____

____

4. How would your life improve if you could set limits without fear or guilt?

____

____

____

____

Jot down your answers in a journal. This process isn't about judging yourself—it's about understanding the stories you've internalized and starting to rewrite them.

How to Set Boundaries that Stick

Setting boundaries can feel daunting, especially if you grew up in an environment where your needs and feelings were routinely dismissed or overshadowed. But boundaries are not only essential—they're liberating. They teach others how to treat you while creating space for you to protect your energy, emotions, and well-being. Let's dive into a simple, step-by-step guide to setting boundaries effectively, followed by real-life examples, strategies, and a reflective exercise to help you get started.

Step 1: Get Clear on What You Need

Before you can set a boundary, you need to understand what it is you're protecting. Maybe it's your time, emotional energy, or personal space. Ask yourself:

- What's draining me right now?

- Where do I feel disrespected or overwhelmed?

- What specific changes would make me feel safer and more at ease?

For example, if you notice that a friend constantly calls you late at night, disrupting your rest, your need might be uninterrupted sleep. Your boundary might be not answering phone calls after 9 PM.

Step 2: Be Specific and Direct

Ambiguity can be a boundary's worst enemy. Vague boundaries like "I need more space" or "Please respect my time" can leave too much room for interpretation. Instead, aim for clarity. For instance:

- Instead of saying, "I'm busy right now," try, "I need 30 minutes of quiet to focus. Let's talk after that."

- Instead of, "Don't interrupt me," try, "If I'm in the middle of working, please wait until I'm done before starting a conversation."

Specificity leaves little room for misunderstanding and increases the likelihood that your boundary will be respected.

Step 3: Use Assertive, Calm Communication

When communicating boundaries, how you say it can be as important as what you say. Assertiveness is key: it's not aggressive, but it's also not apologetic. Using "I" statements helps keep the focus on your needs without blaming others. For example:

- "I feel overwhelmed when I'm interrupted during work. I need uninterrupted time to concentrate."

- "I'm uncomfortable when you comment on my weight. Please don't do that anymore."

A calm, firm tone reinforces your words. Avoid overexplaining or justifying your boundary—your needs are valid as they are.

Step 4: Reinforce Your Boundaries

Unfortunately, some people will test your boundaries. This doesn't mean you're failing; it's an opportunity to reinforce them. Consistency is critical. If someone crosses your boundary, remind them firmly:

- "I've already mentioned that I don't take calls after 9 PM. Let's talk tomorrow instead."

- "I've asked you not to discuss my personal finances. Let's change the subject."

If the behavior continues, follow through with consequences. For instance, if a family member repeatedly criticizes you despite being asked to stop, you might say:

- "If you continue this conversation, I'll need to leave."

- "I won't respond to messages that criticize me. I'll only engage when the discussion is respectful."

Following through shows others that your boundaries are non-negotiable.

Step 5: Start Small and Build Confidence

If the idea of setting boundaries feels overwhelming, start with small, manageable ones. Practice with situations that feel less emotionally charged, like telling a coworker you can't join a meeting or asking a friend not to text during work hours. Each success builds your confidence, making it easier to handle more challenging situations.

Real-Life Examples of Boundary-Setting

With Family:

Scenario: A parent constantly criticizes your life choices.
Boundary: "I appreciate your concern, but I need you to trust my decisions. Let's focus on enjoying our time together instead of discussing this."

With Friends:

Scenario: A friend regularly borrows money and delays repayment.
Boundary: "I'm not comfortable lending money anymore. Let's find other ways to support each other."

At Work:

Scenario: A coworker interrupts you during deep work.
Boundary: "I need to finish this project without distractions. I'll be available to talk at 3 PM."

Reflective Exercise: Practice Your Boundaries

Take a moment to think about a situation in your life where you feel your boundaries are being crossed. Write down:

1. What's happening that makes you uncomfortable?

2. What specific boundary would help you feel more respected?

3. A clear and assertive way to communicate that boundary.

For example:

- Situation: A sibling constantly drops by unannounced.

- Boundary: "I'd appreciate it if you call before visiting."

- Communication: "I love spending time with you, but I need some notice before visits. Please call me ahead of time to see if it works."

Practice saying it aloud until it feels natural.

What to Do When People Push Back

Setting boundaries isn't just a practical decision; it's a deeply personal act of self-respect. It's a declaration to the world—and to yourself—that your time, energy, and emotions have value. But as empowering as it can be to set these limits, it's also one of the hardest things you'll ever do, especially when those closest to you resist. For adult children of narcissists, this resistance can be particularly painful. After years of being conditioned to prioritize others' needs, any pushback can feel like a rejection of your worth.

But here's the truth: pushback isn't about you. It's about the other person's discomfort, fear of change, or loss of control. Understanding why people resist your boundaries—and learning how to navigate their reactions—can help you stay firm and move forward with confidence.

Why People Resist Boundaries

Imagine for a moment that someone rearranged your living room overnight. The sofa is now where the dining table used to be, and your favorite chair is nowhere near the window. Even if the new arrangement is more functional, your initial reaction might be confusion or even frustration. That's how some people feel when you start setting boundaries. They're used to the way things were, and your changes disrupt their expectations.

For those who have benefitted from your lack of boundaries—whether it's through emotional labor, favors, or constant availability—your decision to set limits can feel like a personal loss. Here are a few reasons why pushback happens:

1. **Fear of Losing Control:** For individuals who thrive on control, your newfound assertiveness can feel threatening. They may see your boundaries as a challenge to their authority or influence.

2. **Discomfort with Change:** Humans are creatures of habit, and many people struggle when dynamics shift. Your boundaries might make them question their own behaviors or force them to adapt in ways they're not ready for.

3. **Unresolved Personal Issues:** Often, pushback has little to do with you. It can stem from the other person's insecurities, fear of rejection, or difficulty managing their own emotions.

Recognizing these underlying motivations can help you see resistance for what it is: a reflection of the other person's struggles, not your worth or the validity of your boundaries.

Staying Strong When Others Push Back

When you set boundaries, you're essentially saying, "I value myself enough to protect my well-being." But for someone who's used to you putting their needs first, this can feel like an unwelcome shock. They might react with anger, guilt-tripping, or even accusations of selfishness. This can be incredibly triggering, especially if you've spent years trying to avoid conflict or criticism.

So, how do you stand firm when the pushback comes?

1. **Remember Your Why:** Every boundary you set has a purpose. Maybe it's to protect your mental health, create more time for yourself, or reduce stress. Whatever the reason, keep it front and center. Write it down if you need to, and revisit it whenever you feel yourself wavering.

2. **Stay Calm and Firm:** Pushback often escalates when emotions run high. Responding with calm confidence can diffuse tension and reinforce your position. For example, you might say, "I understand this is hard for you, but this is what I need to feel healthy and balanced."

3. **Avoid Over-Explaining:** It's natural to want to justify your decisions, but too much explaining can weaken your stance and invite arguments. A clear, simple explanation is enough: "This is what works best for me right now."

4. **Anticipate Reactions:** Pushback often comes in predictable forms, such as guilt-tripping ("After all I've done for you...") or playing the victim ("You don't care about me anymore"). Recognize these tactics for what they are—emotional manipulation—and remind yourself that their feelings are not your responsibility.

Coping with the Emotional Fallout

Standing firm can be draining. You might feel guilty, anxious, or even question whether setting boundaries was the right choice. These feelings are normal, but they don't have to derail your progress.

- **Be Kind to Yourself:** Remind yourself that you're not being selfish; you're being healthy. Acknowledge the courage it takes to stand up for your needs, even when it's uncomfortable.

- **Lean on Support:** Whether it's a trusted friend, a therapist, or a support group, sharing your experiences can help you process your emotions and feel less isolated.

- **Practice Self-Care:** Boundary-setting is emotionally taxing, so find ways to recharge. This could be journaling, taking a walk, meditating, or simply spending time doing something you love.

Navigating Tough Conversations

Pushback often leads to difficult conversations. Someone might challenge your boundaries, accuse you of changing, or insist that you're being unfair. These moments can feel like a test of your resolve, but with preparation, you can navigate them effectively.

- **Prepare Your Script:** Before a tough conversation, think about what you want to say and how you'll respond to potential objections. For example: "I know this is different from what you're used to, but I need this boundary to feel balanced and respected."

- **Stay Focused:** Keep the conversation centered on your needs. If the other person tries to deflect or manipulate, gently steer it back to the main point.

- **Recognize Manipulation:** Tactics like guilt-tripping or playing the victim are common, especially for narcissistic individuals. Stay grounded and remember: their reaction is not your responsibility.

Reflect and Practice

Try this exercise: Think of someone in your life who might resist your boundaries. Visualize their likely reaction and practice your response. Write down a few key phrases that affirm your boundary without being confrontational. For example: "I respect your feelings, but this is what I need to do for myself."

Setting boundaries is a bold and brave step, especially when others push back. But every time you hold your ground, you're reinforcing your worth and teaching others how to respect you. It's not easy, but it's worth it. You're not just setting boundaries—you're reclaiming your life. Keep going. You're stronger than you think.

Chapter 6

Finding Compassion for Yourself

You know that voice in your head? The one that never seems satisfied, no matter how hard you try? Maybe it whispers things like, *"You're not good enough,"* or *"Why can't you just get it together?"* It's harsh, relentless, and downright exhausting. If you grew up with a narcissistic parent, that voice likely feels all too familiar—an unwelcome echo of the criticism, judgment, or neglect you faced as a child. It's no wonder you struggle to give yourself grace when it feels like you've spent your whole life being told you don't deserve it.

But here's the truth: You do deserve it. In fact, learning to show yourself compassion is one of the most powerful things you can do to heal from the effects of narcissistic abuse. It's not about excusing your mistakes or ignoring your challenges—it's about recognizing your humanity. It's about treating yourself with the kindness you might readily extend to a dear friend but have been withholding from yourself for far too long.

This chapter is about taking those first steps toward self-compassion. It's not always easy—especially when your inner critic feels like it's in charge—but it's worth it. In the pages ahead, we'll explore how to quiet that critical voice and replace it with one that supports you instead of tearing you down. We'll dive into how to rewrite the stories you've been telling yourself about who you are and what you're capable of, and we'll look at practical ways to nurture yourself emotionally, physically, and spiritually.

Somewhere along the way, you may have been taught that self-compassion is selfish, weak, or indulgent. That's a lie. True compassion isn't about ignoring your flaws or brushing aside accountability—it's about creating a foundation of love and acceptance that allows you to grow, thrive, and reclaim your sense of worth.

This chapter is your invitation to begin that journey. It's not about becoming perfect; it's about learning to be patient with yourself as you heal and embracing the beautiful, imperfect person you've always been. Let's start by silencing that inner critic. You're stronger than you think—and you're worthy of the love you've been so freely giving to everyone else.

Quieting Your Inner Critic

The moment arrives—a chance to try something new, take a bold step, or share an idea close to your heart. But before you can even act, a sharp, familiar voice cuts through your thoughts: *"You'll never pull this off. Why even bother? Everyone will see you're not good enough."* It's relentless, relentless, and leaves you questioning yourself before you've even begun. For many adult children of narcissists, this inner critic is more than just self-doubt. It's an ever-present echo of the past, shaped by years of criticism and impossible expectations, a voice that seems determined to keep you small. But what if you could finally turn the volume down and reclaim your confidence?

That voice, your inner critic, is more than just self-doubt. For many adult children of narcissists, it's an echo of the past—a deeply ingrained narrative formed during years of subtle (or not-so-subtle) criticism, comparison, and manipulation. The inner critic feels like an uninvited guest who moved in long ago, yet still manages to derail your confidence, steal your joy, and question your worth. But here's the truth: you can turn down its volume and, over time, rewrite the script entirely.

Where Your Inner Critic Comes From

To understand your inner critic, it's helpful to trace its origins. If you grew up with a narcissistic parent, chances are you were subjected to a pattern of invalidation, impossible expectations, or outright emotional neglect. Narcissistic parents often project their insecurities onto their children, using criticism or comparison as tools to maintain control.

Perhaps you heard phrases like:

- *"Why can't you be more like your sibling?"*

- *"If you mess this up, you'll embarrass us all."*

- *"Don't get a big head—you're not that special."*

Even moments that should have been joyful—like sharing an accomplishment—were met with dismissal or deflection, teaching you that praise was conditional at best. Over time, these external voices became internalized. They morphed into a mental monologue, constantly replaying every mistake, perceived flaw, or shortcoming.

The inner critic's origins are tied to survival. As a child, aligning with a parent's expectations (even harsh ones) often felt necessary for acceptance or love. But as an adult, this voice no longer serves you. Instead, it keeps you tethered to feelings of inadequacy, fear, and shame.

How Your Inner Critic Affects You

The damage caused by the inner critic isn't just emotional—it's pervasive. Its whispers, often disguised as "truths," shape how you see yourself and interact with the world.

It undermines self-esteem, making it hard to trust your abilities or feel deserving of success. You might overanalyze every decision, afraid of judgment or failure. It can keep you stuck in unhealthy patterns—like perfectionism, people-pleasing, or avoiding risks altogether—because the thought of falling short feels unbearable.

Psychologically, the inner critic reinforces feelings of unworthiness. It's like carrying a constant weight, making you second-guess your worth and potential. For adult children of narcissists, this voice often feels like a lifelong companion, but that doesn't mean it's permanent.

How to Quiet the Inner Critic

Silencing your inner critic doesn't happen overnight, but you can start turning down its volume with intentional practices. The key is not to wage war against it but to approach it with understanding, curiosity, and compassion.

1. Recognize and Name It

The first step in disarming your inner critic is recognizing when it's speaking. Pay attention to the words and tone—it's often sharp, critical, and absolute, using phrases like *"always," "never,"* or *"you can't."*

Give it a name if that helps create some distance. Maybe you call it "the Judge" or "the Naysayer." When it starts up, acknowledge it: *"Oh, there's the Judge again, trying to protect me from failure. Thanks, but I've got this."*

2. Challenge Its Narrative

Your inner critic thrives on unchecked assumptions. Start questioning its claims:

- Is this thought based on facts or fear?

- Would I talk to a loved one the way I'm talking to myself?

- What evidence do I have that contradicts this thought?

For example, if your critic says, *"You'll never get this right,"* counter with, *"I'm still learning, and that's okay. I don't have to be perfect to be worthy."*

3. Reframe Its Role

Rather than seeing your inner critic as an enemy, try reframing it as a misguided protector. Its harshness often stems from a desire to shield you from disappointment or rejection. By acknowledging its intention without accepting its tactics, you can say, *"I see what you're trying to do, but I don't need that kind of protection anymore."*

4. Practice Self-Compassion

The antidote to the inner critic is self-compassion. Treat yourself with the same kindness you'd offer a close friend. Replace harsh judgments with supportive affirmations, like:

- *"I'm allowed to make mistakes—they're part of growth."*

- *"My worth isn't tied to what I achieve."*

- *"I'm doing the best I can, and that's enough."*

Repeat these affirmations often, even if they feel awkward at first. Over time, they can replace the critic's voice with one that uplifts rather than tears down.

Reflective Exercise: Rewriting the Script

1. **Identify Your Inner Critic's Messages**

   Take 10 minutes to jot down common phrases or criticisms your inner voice repeats. Be honest and specific.

2. Challenge Each Criticism

Next to each message, write a compassionate response. If the critic says, *"You're not good at anything,"* your response might be, *"That's not true—I've overcome challenges before, and I'm capable of learning and growing."*

____

____

____

____

____

____

____

____

____

3. **Practice Daily Affirmations**

Choose one or two affirmations to focus on each day. Write them down, say them out loud, or post them where you'll see them often.

____

____

____

____

____

____

____

Your inner critic may have been part of your story for a long time, but it doesn't have to define your future. By recognizing its origins, challenging its messages, and practicing self-compassion, you can begin to quiet its voice and replace it with one that's gentler, kinder, and more empowering.

Healing is a journey, and every small step you take—every moment you choose to speak to yourself with love—is progress. You deserve to live free from the shadows of the past and embrace a life where your inner voice cheers you on instead of holding you back.

Letting Go of Limiting Labels and Lies

One of the most powerful truths about healing is this: you are not defined by the narrative handed to you by others. The story your narcissistic parent told about who you are—whether through their words, actions, or the silence of neglect—is not the full story. You have the power to change it. No matter how deeply rooted those old labels and lies may feel, you can choose to rewrite your narrative and embrace a version of yourself that reflects your true worth, strength, and potential.

For many adult children of narcissists, the narratives they carry often sound like this: *I'm too much. I'm not enough. I'll never be loved for who I am. If I don't please others, I'll lose their approval.* These beliefs aren't just fleeting thoughts; they become ingrained as core truths, shaping how you see yourself and interact with the world. These self-beliefs didn't appear out of nowhere. They were built, brick by brick, through years of gaslighting, criticism, conditional love, and emotional invalidation. And while you didn't choose to inherit these beliefs, you do have the power to challenge and change them.

Recognizing the Narratives Holding You Back

To rewrite your story, you must first identify the old one. Start by examining the words and ideas you've been carrying about yourself. Ask yourself:

- What did I believe about myself as a child?

- What labels did my parent(s) or caregiver(s) impose on me?

- How do those beliefs affect the way I see myself today?

Perhaps you were labeled as the "selfish one" whenever you asserted a need or desire. Maybe you were told you were too sensitive whenever you expressed pain. These labels can lodge themselves deep in your psyche, subtly guiding how you show up in the world. Over time, they form a narrative that keeps you small, cautious, or overly critical of yourself.

It's important to understand that these beliefs aren't facts—they're distortions. They were tools used by your parent to control or diminish you, but they were never about your true character. Recognizing this distinction is the first step in breaking free from their grip.

Reframing Negative Beliefs

Once you've identified the negative narratives, it's time to challenge and reframe them. This process isn't about ignoring or denying the pain you've endured—it's about reclaiming your voice and choosing a more empowering truth.

Here's an example: Let's say you've internalized the belief, *I'm selfish if I prioritize my needs*. This belief likely came from years of being made to feel guilty for putting yourself first, even when it was necessary. To reframe it, you might write: *My needs are valid, and taking care of myself allows me to be my best for others.* Notice how this shift doesn't just reject the old belief—it replaces it with something healthier and more affirming.

Another common narrative might be, *I'm unlovable because my parent didn't value me.* Reframing this could look like: *My worth isn't defined by anyone's inability to see it. I am deserving of love and respect just as I am.* These reframes aren't about pretending the past didn't happen; they're about refusing to let it dictate your future.

Crafting Your New Story

Rewriting your story isn't just about rejecting the old—it's about actively creating a new, positive self-concept that aligns with who you truly are. Start by asking yourself:

- Who do I want to be?

- What strengths have I developed because of my experiences?

- How do I want to see myself moving forward?

Write this vision down as a declaration. It doesn't have to be perfect, and it may evolve over time, but let it serve as a guiding light. For instance, you might write: *I am a resilient, compassionate person who is learning to trust and love myself. My past shaped me, but it doesn't define me. I am worthy of joy, connection, and fulfillment.*

Learning from Real-Life Transformations

Take Maria's story, for example. Maria grew up in a household where her mother constantly criticized her appearance and compared her to others. By her mid-30s, Maria struggled with low self-esteem and an obsessive need for external validation. Through therapy and self-reflection, Maria realized her narrative—*I'm not enough unless I prove my worth*—wasn't her truth but a reflection of her mother's insecurities.

Maria began rewriting her story by practicing affirmations like: *I am enough as I am. My value isn't tied to how others perceive me.* She also surrounded herself with people who uplifted and valued her for who she was. Over time, Maria found that the old narrative lost its power, and her new self-concept—confident, independent, and self-assured—began to take root.

Reflective Exercises to Help You Rewrite Your Story

1. **Name the Old Lies:** Take a moment to list the negative beliefs or labels you've internalized from your upbringing. Write them down.

2. **Challenge and Reframe:** For each belief, write a positive, affirming statement that counters it. Use language that feels authentic and empowering to you.

3. **Create Your New Narrative:** Write a short paragraph or journal entry about who you are becoming. Focus on your strengths, values, and the life you're building for yourself.

4. **Practice Daily Affirmations:** Choose one or two affirmations from your new narrative and say

them aloud every morning. Visualize yourself living out these truths.

Visualizing Your Empowered Self

Take a few minutes each day to imagine your future self—confident, self-assured, and free from the weight of old narratives. Picture how this version of you walks, talks, and interacts with others. Visualization is a powerful tool for rewiring your brain and reinforcing your new story.

As you begin to rewrite your story, remember this: it's a process, not a one-time event. Be patient with yourself. Every time you challenge an old belief or affirm a new truth, you're taking a step toward freedom and self-empowerment. You are the author of your story now, and the possibilities are endless.

Taking Care of You

Let's face it: Self-care can feel like an alien concept, especially if you were raised in an environment where taking care of your own needs wasn't just overlooked—it was actively discouraged. Perhaps you grew up learning that the only way to earn love and approval was by prioritizing others' needs above your own. Maybe you were taught to be "the strong one," the one who always gives, sacrifices, and puts everyone else's comfort first. Over time, you may have internalized the idea that your own needs didn't matter, or worse, that taking time for yourself was selfish or indulgent.

This pattern is all too familiar for many adult children of narcissistic parents. For years, you might have felt invisible or unworthy of attention, silently carrying the weight of your family's emotional needs. You might have felt like you were the one responsible for keeping things running smoothly, whether it was managing the chaos or trying to maintain peace at any cost. But somewhere along the way, you lost sight of yourself. The person who mattered the most—YOU—became an afterthought.

If you're nodding along, you're not alone. It's not unusual for adult children of narcissistic parents to struggle with self-care because we've been conditioned to put ourselves last. The challenge, however, is that neglecting yourself for too long can take a toll. Not just emotionally, but physically, mentally, and spiritually. Your body and mind can only take so much before it starts to show up in ways you can no longer ignore— fatigue, anxiety, irritability, and even physical ailments. When you're constantly giving, eventually there's nothing left to give. This is where self-care becomes not just a luxury, but an absolute necessity for your healing.

Why Self-Care is Essential for Healing

Self-care is often mistaken for pampering or indulgence, but it's so much more than that. For someone like you, who has spent much of their life prioritizing others, self-care is an act of **self-respect** and **self-love**. It's about recognizing that you matter, that your well-being is just as important as anyone else's, and that you deserve to feel whole, healthy, and happy. Taking care of yourself isn't selfish; it's essential for healing, growth, and ultimately, becoming the best version of yourself.

The healing process from narcissistic abuse isn't linear, and it can often feel like a slow climb. Self-care helps ease the burden, providing you with the emotional and physical energy to keep moving forward. When you take the time to nurture yourself, you're also sending a powerful message to your subconscious: **You are worthy of care.** It's a form of reclaiming the love and attention that may have been denied to you in the past. Through self-care, you can gradually rebuild the sense of self that was undermined by narcissistic parenting.

Practical Tips for Self-Care

Now, let's talk about how to actually **start** taking care of yourself. It may feel daunting at first, especially if you've spent years neglecting your needs. But the key is to start small and build consistency. Here are some practical tips to help you incorporate self-care into your daily life:

1. Physical Self-Care: Nourish Your Body

Taking care of your body is an essential part of healing. This doesn't mean you have to sign up for an intense workout routine or overhaul your entire diet. Start with simple changes that make you feel good.

- **Get Moving:** Physical activity doesn't have to be intense. Even a short walk, stretching, or yoga can help release built-up tension and boost your mood.

- **Eat Mindfully:** Nourish your body with healthy, balanced meals. Pay attention to how certain foods make you feel—choose those that energize you rather than drain you.

- **Sleep Well:** Rest is crucial for emotional and physical recovery. Create a calming bedtime routine, and aim for 7–9 hours of sleep a night.

2. Emotional Self-Care: Tend to Your Heart

Caring for your emotions means acknowledging how you feel and giving yourself permission to experience those feelings without judgment.

- **Journaling:** Writing can be an incredibly therapeutic way to process your emotions. Try setting aside a few minutes each day to reflect on your thoughts and feelings.

- **Practice Gratitude:** Shifting your focus toward what you're thankful for can help reframe negative thoughts. Start a gratitude journal, noting three things you're grateful for each day.

- **Connect with Others:** Isolation can be a byproduct of narcissistic abuse, but healthy relationships are a key part of self-care. Seek out supportive friends, groups, or a therapist who can offer understanding and validation.

3. Mental Self-Care: Clear the Clutter

Your mind has likely been through a lot, and it's important to create space for clarity and calm.

- **Meditation or Mindfulness:** Practicing mindfulness helps you stay present, reducing the overwhelming effects of anxiety and stress. Even just a few minutes a day can make a significant difference.

- **Limit Negative Inputs:** If certain people, media, or environments trigger negative thoughts or emotions, set boundaries and limit your exposure to them. You deserve peace of mind.

- **Set Boundaries:** It's essential to create mental space by setting boundaries with others—whether it's limiting time with toxic individuals or saying no to things that drain you.

Consistency is Key

The most important part of self-care isn't just starting—it's **sticking with it**. It's easy to fall back into old habits of putting yourself last, especially when you've spent so much time taking care of others. But consistency is what transforms self-care from an occasional luxury to a regular practice that sustains your emotional health and healing.

Treat self-care as a non-negotiable part of your day, like brushing your teeth or getting enough sleep. It might feel uncomfortable at first, especially if you've been conditioned to feel guilty for taking time for yourself. But remember, self-care isn't selfish—it's a vital act of self-respect.

Reflective Exercise: Creating Your Personal Self-Care Plan

To help you stay on track, take a moment to reflect on your own self-care needs. What makes you feel nurtured, rested, and supported? Write down your answers and create a personalized self-care plan. Include physical, emotional, and mental practices that resonate with you.

Once you have your plan, commit to integrating at least one of these practices into your routine every day, even if it's just for 10 minutes. As you start to track your progress, notice how your emotional and physical state improves over time. Reflect on the benefits you experience and celebrate each step forward.

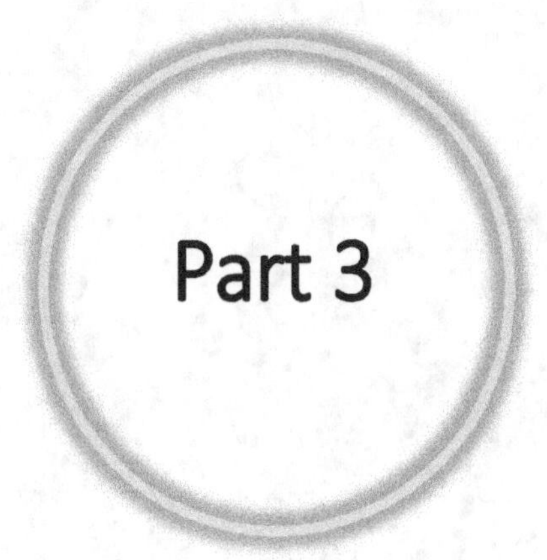

CREATING A LIFE YOU LOVE

Moving from Surviving to Thriving

Chapter 7

Healing Relationships One Step at a Time

Growing up with a narcissistic parent often means navigating a maze of complex emotions when it comes to relationships. As you begin to heal, you might find yourself grappling with the painful yet inevitable question: *What about the relationships that still have a hold on me?* Maybe it's a parent, a sibling, or even a friend who doesn't fully understand the boundaries you've set or the changes you've made. You may feel conflicted, torn between the desire to heal old wounds and the instinct to protect yourself from further hurt. It's an emotional tightrope that many adult children of narcissists walk, longing for connection while also needing space to protect your newfound peace. Rebuilding these relationships can feel daunting, but it's possible to approach them with clarity and intention, recognizing what's worth saving and what might be better left behind.

If this scenario resonates with you, you're not alone. Many adult children of narcissistic parents grapple with the emotional conflict of wanting to rebuild relationships while also needing to protect themselves from further hurt. The very people who were supposed to nurture and support you often become the ones who make you feel unworthy, invalid, or invisible. As you navigate your healing journey, it's only natural to question: *How do I rebuild relationships with people who've caused so much pain?* It's a question that doesn't have an easy answer, but it is possible to approach these relationships with intention, healing, and clarity.

This chapter is here to guide you through one of the most complex parts of your recovery: healing relationships. Rebuilding connections after growing up with a narcissistic parent isn't about fixing everything or expecting things to go back to "normal." It's about understanding what's possible, learning to navigate forgiveness on your terms, and creating connections that allow you to thrive emotionally—whether that means mending old wounds or, sometimes, letting go of relationships that no longer serve you.

In the following pages, we'll explore how to make important decisions about which relationships to invest in, how to approach forgiveness—both for yourself and others—and how to build healthier, more authentic connections moving forward. You'll find insights, strategies, and personal stories to help you navigate this journey with empathy, understanding, and confidence. Remember, this chapter isn't about forcing you to reconcile with everyone in your life. It's about helping you find a balance that allows you to heal, grow, and create a life full of healthy relationships that support your emotional well-being. It's time to reclaim the power to shape your connections in a way that reflects who you truly are.

Who Deserves a Seat at Your Table?

Think for a moment about the people in your life. Who do you feel uplifted and supported by? And who leaves you feeling drained, unworthy, or anxious? In this journey of healing, it's crucial to take a step back and reflect on the relationships that truly nourish you versus those that harm or hinder your growth. As an adult child of narcissists, your ability to assess and evaluate these relationships may be clouded by past emotional manipulation or a history of mistaking toxicity for love. But now, you have the power to choose who gets a seat at your table.

When deciding which relationships to rebuild and which to release, it's important to consider a few key factors. First, **mutual respect** is essential. Healthy relationships are built on a foundation of respect, where both parties value each other's opinions, needs, and boundaries. If you're the one always giving while receiving little or no respect in return, it may be time to reassess. Healthy connections are reciprocal—both parties invest in the relationship and feel valued.

Next, look at **support**. Do the people in your life encourage your growth and well-being, or do they seem to drain your energy and self-worth? Real support is not about rescuing or fixing but about being present, encouraging your dreams, and standing with you through struggles. If someone consistently undermines your efforts or belittles your feelings, it's worth questioning whether they truly deserve a space in your life.

Finally, **emotional safety** is a non-negotiable. You should feel safe to express yourself, your needs, and your emotions without fear of judgment, manipulation, or retaliation. If a relationship leaves you feeling on edge, constantly walking on eggshells, or if your emotions are regularly invalidated, it might be time to release that connection.

Evaluating relationships objectively can be tough, especially if you've been taught to ignore your feelings in favor of others' needs. Start by looking at **past behaviors**. How have the people around you treated you in the past? Were they supportive, or did they take advantage of your kindness and vulnerability? Pay attention to **current dynamics**. Are you still in the same unhealthy patterns, or is there room for growth and change? And don't forget about **the potential for positive change**. People can grow and evolve, but the question is whether they are willing to put in the effort for a healthier dynamic with you.

Letting go of relationships can be one of the most painful steps in your healing journey. The grief that comes with releasing someone you once cared for—or who may still hold a role in your life—can be overwhelming. You might feel guilty, sad, or even fearful of the unknown. These emotions are valid. But it's important to remember that, just like healing, letting go is a process. It may hurt now, but in time, it will bring you closer to the peace, freedom, and self-respect you deserve.

To help you through this process, take some time for reflection. Ask yourself: Which relationships bring me peace and strength? Which ones consistently drain me or make me feel less than? Journal your thoughts and feelings—sometimes writing things down can give clarity and release. You may even want to make two lists: one for relationships worth investing in and another for those that no longer serve you. In doing this, you'll begin to see the patterns, and slowly but surely, you'll create the space to fill your life with those who truly support and respect you.

As you navigate this process, remember—you are worthy of relationships that honor your growth, your emotional needs, and your inherent value. Take the time to choose wisely who gets to be part of your life, and above all, trust yourself. You have the wisdom to recognize the difference between those who uplift you and those who hold you back.

When to Forgive (and When to Walk Away)

Forgiveness is one of the most complex and misunderstood aspects of healing. For adult children of narcissists, the concept often feels tangled in societal expectations, religious teachings, or family pressure. You may have been told, "You must forgive them—they're still your parent," or even that forgiveness is the only way to truly heal. But let's pause here and unpack that notion. While forgiveness can be freeing, it's not a one-size-fits-all solution, and it certainly doesn't require you to subject yourself to continued harm or an unchanging relationship.

At its core, forgiveness is a deeply personal choice. It's about releasing the hold someone's actions have on your emotional state, allowing you to move forward. But here's the catch: forgiveness doesn't have to mean reconciliation. It's entirely possible—and valid—to forgive someone in your heart without inviting them back into your life. For adult children of narcissists, this distinction is crucial. Narcissistic parents often resist accountability, making genuine reconciliation difficult or even impossible. Forgiveness, in this context, is not about excusing or forgetting their behavior. Instead, it's about reclaiming your peace and emotional autonomy.

Forgiving for Your Peace vs. Forgiving for the Relationship

Many people feel obligated to forgive as a way to fix or maintain relationships, especially with family members. You might hear messages like, "Families are forever," or "You'll regret cutting ties one day." But let's be honest: not every relationship is salvageable, and not every person is willing—or capable—of change. Forgiving for your peace is about freeing yourself from the bitterness or resentment that may weigh you down. It's a gift you give yourself, not the other person.

On the other hand, forgiving to preserve a relationship is a choice that comes with conditions. Is the other person genuinely remorseful? Are they willing to work on their behavior and make amends? Are they creating a safe and respectful environment for you to reconnect? If the answer to these questions is no, then forgiving for the sake of the relationship might lead to further disappointment and emotional harm.

When Forgiveness Might Be Right—and When It's Time to Walk Away

So how do you decide? Here's a framework to help you evaluate:

1. **The Other Person's Willingness to Change:** Are they capable of acknowledging the harm they've caused? Have they shown a consistent effort to improve their behavior? Genuine change requires accountability and action, not just empty apologies.

2. **The Impact on Your Well-Being:** Does maintaining the relationship make you feel more anxious, drained, or unsafe? Healing requires protecting your peace and prioritizing your mental health, even if it means creating distance.

3. **The Potential for Future Harm:** Is there a risk that continuing the relationship could lead to more emotional damage? Patterns of manipulation, gaslighting, or toxic behavior rarely disappear without significant effort from the person responsible.

Choosing to walk away isn't about being unforgiving—it's about honoring your worth and recognizing that some relationships are too harmful to sustain. Letting go can be one of the most loving decisions you make for yourself.

Navigating the Emotional Complexity of Forgiveness

Let's be real: forgiveness isn't easy. It's not a magical moment where everything feels resolved, nor is it always linear. You may forgive someone in your heart today, only to find yourself grappling with anger or sadness tomorrow. That's okay. The process is messy, but it's also an opportunity to grow.

Start with self-compassion. Remind yourself that whatever choice you make—whether to forgive or to walk away—you're doing your best with the information and emotions you have right now. Allow yourself to feel the full range of emotions, from anger to grief to relief.

Setting boundaries is another critical part of navigating forgiveness. Whether you choose to maintain a relationship or not, boundaries protect your emotional space and help you establish what is and isn't acceptable moving forward. If you're forgiving but still engaging with the person, make it clear what needs to change and what will happen if those changes aren't respected.

Finally, don't hesitate to seek support. Talk to a trusted friend, join a support group, or work with a therapist who understands narcissistic family dynamics. These allies can help you process your feelings and stay grounded in your decisions.

Reflective Exercise: Forgiveness vs. Walking Away

Take some time to reflect on the relationships in your life. Ask yourself:

- Is this person willing to take responsibility for their actions?

- How does their presence affect my emotional well-being?

- Do I feel safe and respected in this relationship?

Write down your thoughts in a journal or talk them through with someone you trust. If you're considering walking away, list three ways this decision could bring you peace. Then list three small steps you can take to begin creating that distance.

Self-Care as You Decide

Whether you choose forgiveness, walking away, or a mix of both, remember to care for yourself during this process. Engage in activities that replenish your energy and nurture your spirit—whether it's journaling, meditating, spending time in nature, or simply resting. Healing is a journey, and every step forward is worth celebrating.

Forgiveness is a powerful tool, but it's not a demand. It's an option you get to choose—or not—based on what serves your well-being. And whether you forgive, walk away, or find peace somewhere in between, the most important thing is this: you have the right to prioritize your emotional health and live a life free from the shadows of the past.

Building Better Connections

Relationships are the heart of our lives, and no matter what your past has looked like, it's never too late to create healthier, more fulfilling connections. This chapter is all about hope—hope that you can break the patterns of dysfunction, hope that you can experience relationships grounded in mutual respect and care, and hope that you can find joy in being authentically yourself with others. Building better connections isn't about perfection; it's about progress, and every small step forward matters.

The Pillars of Healthy Relationships

Healthy relationships don't happen by accident; they're built on a foundation of trust, respect, and emotional safety. For adult children of narcissists, these pillars might feel foreign, even unattainable at first. But as you start to understand and practice these components, you'll find that they form the bedrock of meaningful and fulfilling connections.

One key element is **mutual respect**—the ability to value each other's thoughts, feelings, and boundaries without trying to control or manipulate. In contrast to the one-sided dynamics you may have experienced growing up, mutual respect creates an even playing field where both parties feel seen and valued.

Open communication is another cornerstone. This doesn't mean sharing everything about your life but being honest, clear, and willing to listen. It's about expressing your needs without fear of judgment and being open to hearing others' perspectives, even when they differ from your own.

Healthy relationships are also characterized by **emotional support.** This means being there for each other during tough times and celebrating the wins together. For someone who has been conditioned to suppress their feelings or prioritize others' needs, giving and receiving emotional support can feel daunting. But when nurtured, it becomes one of the most rewarding aspects of connection.

Finally, **shared values and mutual goals** strengthen bonds over time. These might include similar outlooks on honesty, family, or personal growth. While differences can exist, having shared values fosters alignment and long-term harmony.

Practical Steps to Build and Maintain Better Relationships

Building healthy relationships starts with small, actionable steps. Here are some ways to begin transforming the way you connect:

1. **Improve Your Communication Skills:** Clear and respectful communication is a learned skill, especially if you've grown up in an environment where conversations were filled with manipulation or criticism. Start by practicing active listening—truly focusing on what the other person is saying instead of planning your response. Use "I" statements, such as, "I feel upset when..." to express your feelings without blaming or attacking.

2. **Set and Respect Boundaries:** Boundaries are essential for maintaining emotional safety. Think of them as the invisible lines that define what's okay and what's not in your relationships. For example, you might decide that you won't tolerate being yelled at during a disagreement or that you need alone time to recharge. Communicating these boundaries clearly—and respecting others'

boundaries in return—builds mutual trust and respect.

3. **Show Appreciation and Empathy:** Take time to notice the positive contributions of the people in your life and express your gratitude. Simple acts, like thanking a friend for their support or complimenting a partner on their kindness, go a long way in strengthening bonds. Equally important is empathy—the ability to understand and share someone else's feelings. This doesn't mean fixing their problems but showing that you care and are willing to listen.

The Role of Self-Awareness in Better Connections

Healthy relationships aren't just about what you bring to the table; they're also about how you show up for yourself. Self-awareness is a critical piece of the puzzle. When you understand your triggers, needs, and emotional patterns, you're better equipped to engage with others in a way that feels authentic and fulfilling.

Personal growth is an ongoing journey, and every step you take toward healing enhances your capacity for connection. Whether it's learning to manage conflict without shutting down, confronting the fear of abandonment, or embracing vulnerability, the work you do on yourself will ripple outward into your relationships.

Reflective Exercise: Charting Your Path to Healthier Connections

Take a few moments to reflect on your current relationships. Ask yourself:

- Which relationships feel healthy and supportive? What makes them work well?

____

____

____

____

____

____

____

____

- Are there any connections that feel draining or unbalanced? Why do you think that is?

____

____

____

____

____

____

____

____

- What's one small step you can take today to improve a specific relationship?

____

____

____

____

Now, write down an action plan. For example, if you feel disconnected from a friend, you might decide to reach out and schedule a catch-up. If a relationship feels unbalanced, you might practice setting a boundary, such as declining a request that feels overwhelming.

As you work on building better connections, remember that change takes time. Celebrate the small wins, like having an open conversation or standing firm in a boundary. Forgive yourself for missteps, and understand that growth isn't linear—it's a series of steps forward, backward, and sideways. The key is to keep moving forward, trusting that each effort brings you closer to the meaningful relationships you deserve.

Healthy relationships are possible for you. You don't need to carry the weight of past patterns forever. As you lean into connection with yourself and others, you'll find that the bonds you create are not just stronger but richer and more rewarding than you ever imagined.

Chapter 8

Finding Your Voice and Living Your Truth

For years, you may have felt like your thoughts and opinions didn't count. Perhaps every time you tried to express yourself, your words were dismissed, twisted, or ignored. Over time, you learned it was easier—and safer—to stay silent. The habits of self-censorship, people-pleasing, and putting others' needs above your own became second nature. Yet deep down, a part of you has always longed to be heard, understood, and valued.

Growing up with a narcissistic parent often means living in a world where someone else's voice drowns out your own. Your needs, feelings, and preferences were overshadowed by their demands, leaving little room for you to figure out who you truly are. Now, as an adult, reclaiming your voice can feel both overwhelming and unfamiliar. It might even stir up guilt or fear—what if speaking up causes conflict or rejection? These feelings are valid, but they don't have to control you anymore.

This chapter marks a turning point in your healing journey. Finding your voice is about more than speaking your mind; it's about reconnecting with your authentic self. It's the process of rediscovering the person you were always meant to be before your identity became shaped by someone else's expectations and control. It's about taking back your power and living a life that feels right for *you*.

Reclaiming your voice may feel like learning a new language at first, but it's one of the most empowering steps you'll take. You deserve to express your desires, set your boundaries, and pursue the things that light you up without apology.

In this chapter, we'll explore how to start taking control of your life—one step at a time. You'll learn how to identify what you truly want, rediscover passions and hobbies that bring you joy, and build the courage to embrace your authentic self. Along the way, we'll share real-life stories of others who have walked this path, and you'll find practical exercises to help you break free from the silence that has held you back.

This is your moment to step into the light, let your voice be heard, and live boldly and unapologetically. Let's take that first step together.

Taking Back Control of Your Life

Life with a narcissistic parent often feels like navigating a maze with no clear exit. You might find yourself frozen in indecision over the simplest choices, wondering if you'll ever be "good enough" to make the right call. Maybe it's the paralyzing anxiety of picking an outfit, a meal, or even a career path, always haunted by the fear of judgment or failure. These moments, small or big, reflect the deeper struggle of living under someone else's control for so long. For many adult children of narcissists, the idea of steering their own lives feels both liberating and terrifying—a skill they were never taught but desperately need to learn.

Growing up under the shadow of a narcissistic parent often means you weren't given the space to explore who you are or what you want. Maybe you were told what to wear, what to like, even what to think. Perhaps your attempts to assert independence were met with ridicule or guilt-tripping. Over time, it can leave you feeling as though your choices don't matter—or worse, that you're incapable of making good ones. But here's the truth: Taking back control of your life is not only possible; it's essential. It's the first step toward becoming the person you've always been meant to be.

Why Your Choices Matter

Taking back control starts with recognizing that your choices *do* matter—because they're yours. For so long, you may have been living someone else's script, trying to meet expectations that were never truly yours to begin with. The decisions you make, no matter how small, are a way to honor your unique perspective and desires. When you allow yourself to dream, set goals, and follow through on what truly matters to you, you're affirming your worth and reclaiming the autonomy that may have been denied to you for years.

But let's be real: This isn't easy. After years of being told—directly or indirectly—that your decisions are wrong or unimportant, it's natural to feel hesitant, even paralyzed. You might question whether your instincts can be trusted. The good news is that learning to trust yourself is like building a muscle. It takes practice, but every step forward makes you stronger.

Starting Small, Dreaming Big

If the idea of taking control feels overwhelming, begin with small, everyday decisions. Give yourself permission to choose what you want for dinner, what movie to watch, or how you'll spend your weekend. These seemingly minor choices build the confidence needed to tackle bigger decisions down the road.

At the same time, reconnect with the dreams you may have pushed aside. Ask yourself: *What do I truly want in life?* Maybe you've always wanted to go back to school, change careers, or travel the world. Or perhaps your dream is as simple—and as profound—as creating a home filled with love and safety. Whatever it is, this is your chance to give it the attention it deserves.

To help clarify your dreams, try this exercise: Set aside time to write down everything you'd pursue if fear or judgment weren't holding you back. Let it flow without censoring yourself. Once you have your list, pick one goal that excites you most. That's where your journey begins.

Creating a Plan for Your Goals

Dreams are powerful, but they need a plan to become reality. Break down your chosen goal into smaller, manageable steps. For example, if your dream is to start a new career, your first step might be researching courses or certifications. Next, set a timeline and prioritize these steps. Celebrate each milestone, no matter how small, as a victory.

It's also helpful to create a visual reminder of your goals. A vision board—a collage of images and words representing your dreams—can inspire you on tough days. Or keep a journal where you track your progress and reflect on how far you've come. These tools serve as tangible proof that you're in charge of your life now.

Facing the Fear of Independence

Fear is a natural part of this process. You might worry about making mistakes or disappointing others. But remember: Mistakes are just opportunities to learn, and your life isn't about pleasing everyone else anymore. Building self-confidence takes time, so be patient with yourself.

One way to combat fear is to practice listening to your instincts. Start with low-stakes situations, like deciding which book to read next. Over time, you'll begin to recognize that inner voice—the one that's been quieted for so long—and learn to trust it.

Another strategy is to surround yourself with supportive people who encourage your independence. Whether it's friends, a therapist, or an online community, having cheerleaders on your journey makes all the difference.

Reflecting on Your Next Steps

To wrap up, take some time to think about what taking control means to you personally. Ask yourself:

1. *What's one area of my life where I feel ready to make a change?*

____

____

____

____

____

____

____

2. *What's holding me back, and how can I overcome it?*

____

____

____

____

____

____

3. *What small step can I take today to move closer to my goals?*

____

____

____

____

____

Write down your answers and revisit them often. They're a roadmap to the life you're building—a life where you call the shots and finally feel free.

Taking back control of your life isn't about getting it all right the first time. It's about showing up for yourself, one decision at a time. And with each choice you make, you're proving to yourself that you are capable, deserving, and unstoppable.

Doing What Makes You Happy

Imagine a version of yourself where joy isn't a distant dream or a fleeting moment but a steady, comforting presence woven into the fabric of your daily life. This version of you exists—it's real and reachable. The key lies in reconnecting with the activities and pursuits that genuinely light up your soul. Happiness, true happiness, is not selfish or indulgent. It's the fuel that keeps you resilient, the spark that reminds you life can be more than survival—it can be fulfilling.

For adult children of narcissists, however, the concept of pursuing personal happiness often feels foreign or even risky. Growing up in a home dominated by a narcissistic parent may have meant that your needs, desires, and interests were either dismissed, belittled, or treated as secondary to theirs. In many cases, you might have been subtly—or not so subtly—conditioned to seek validation and approval from others before allowing yourself to pursue what you enjoyed. Perhaps you were told that your dreams were impractical, your hobbies were a waste of time, or that your achievements weren't enough to earn praise. Over time, you may have internalized these messages, learning to prioritize what others wanted for you over what you truly wanted for yourself.

But here's the thing: you don't have to live in that space anymore. The past shaped you, yes, but it doesn't have to define your future. Reclaiming happiness means rediscovering what makes your heart sing without needing anyone else's permission. It's about stepping out of the shadow of validation and standing confidently in your own light.

Rediscovering Your Joy

Start by asking yourself a simple but powerful question: *What brings me joy?* The answer might not come immediately, and that's okay. For many adult children of narcissists, the years spent putting others first can leave you feeling disconnected from your own interests and passions. This is your chance to reconnect. Think back to a time—perhaps in childhood, before things became complicated—when you felt pure, unbridled joy. Was it painting, playing an instrument, reading, writing stories, running, dancing, or building things? Did you lose hours creating something, exploring nature, or imagining new worlds?

If revisiting old hobbies doesn't resonate, try exploring new ones. Give yourself permission to experiment. Take a class in something you've always been curious about, join a local group centered on an activity, or simply try something you've never done before, like gardening, crafting, or hiking. The beauty of this process is that it's yours—there's no right or wrong way to find what makes you happy.

Making Space for Happiness

Life is busy, and it can feel like there's no time for anything beyond responsibilities. But carving out space for what you love isn't just important—it's essential. Start small. Dedicate 15 minutes a day or an hour a week to a hobby or activity that excites you. Treat this time as non-negotiable, just like you would a meeting or an appointment.

Look for ways to integrate your passions into your daily life. For instance, if you enjoy writing, start journaling in the mornings or evenings. If you love art, set up a small creative corner in your home. If you thrive on connection, join a group or community where you can share your interests with like-minded people. Sometimes, pursuing happiness means creating the environment that nurtures it.

A Simple Reflective Exercise

Take a moment to sit down with a pen and paper or a journal. Write out the following prompts and answer them thoughtfully:

1. What activities or hobbies have brought me joy in the past?

____

____

____

____

____

____

2. What new activities have I always been curious about but never tried?

____

____

____

____

3. How do I feel when I imagine myself engaging in these activities?

____

____

____

____

____

4. What is one small step I can take today to bring more of these into my life?

If you're not sure where to start, pick one activity—any activity—that catches your eye. Try it for a week and pay attention to how it makes you feel. Do you feel lighter, more energized, or more at peace? If so, keep going. If not, give yourself grace and move on to something else. The goal isn't to master a skill or impress anyone—it's simply to explore and enjoy.

The Power of Community

Finding supportive people who share your interests can make the journey even richer. Whether it's joining a book club, an online group, or a local class, connecting with others who value the same things can inspire you and help you stay committed. These communities can also provide the encouragement and validation you may have lacked growing up.

Remember, happiness isn't just an end goal—it's a practice. By rediscovering what makes you happy and creating space for it in your life, you're reclaiming a part of yourself that was overlooked for far too long. Each step you take toward joy, no matter how small, is a step toward healing and wholeness. You deserve this. Always.

Becoming the Real You

Let's say for instance you are standing at a fork in the road. On one path lies the familiar terrain of people-pleasing, self-doubt, and quiet despair—the life you've known, shaped by the expectations and judgments of others. The other path is unknown but promising. It's where you finally let yourself step out from the shadows, honor your desires, and embrace the person you were always meant to be. This is the journey of becoming your real self.

Take Maya, for instance. Raised by a father who was hypercritical and a mother who seemed to only approve when she excelled, Maya spent years perfecting the art of being who everyone else wanted her to be. She became the dependable one, the peacemaker, and the overachiever. Yet inside, she felt lost and hollow. It wasn't until her mid-30s, after a particularly painful breakup, that she realized something had to change. For the first time, Maya began asking herself questions she'd avoided her whole life: *What do I want? What makes me happy?* Slowly but surely, she began to shed the layers of "shoulds" and "musts" that had been imposed on her. Today, Maya speaks of a newfound lightness in her step. She paints, sings, and unapologetically says "no" when she needs to. The transformation didn't happen overnight, but it has allowed her to step into a life that feels genuine and fulfilling.

For many adult children of narcissists, the idea of embracing your true self can feel foreign, even scary. Growing up, you might have learned that being authentic meant risking rejection, disapproval, or even ridicule. Perhaps you were taught that your feelings, dreams, and preferences didn't matter—or worse, that they were "wrong." This conditioning often leads to a life of suppressing who you are in favor of meeting others' expectations. The result? A quiet, gnawing sense that something isn't right, a persistent ache to be seen and valued for who you truly are.

But here's the truth: embracing your authentic self isn't selfish—it's revolutionary. It's a declaration to the world that you will no longer diminish yourself to fit into molds that others created for you. It's about reclaiming your identity and stepping into the freedom and empowerment of being unapologetically you. When you allow yourself to live authentically, you unlock a wellspring of inner peace, creativity, and connection that has likely been stifled for too long.

Letting Go of Fear

One of the biggest obstacles to embracing your true self is the fear of judgment or rejection. It's natural to worry about how others might react when you stop being the person they expect you to be. However, living in fear of others' opinions is like being a bird who never leaves its cage, even when the door is wide open. True freedom comes when you begin to prioritize your own approval over anyone else's.

Start small. The next time you catch yourself holding back an opinion or stifling your preferences to avoid conflict, pause and ask yourself: *What would happen if I spoke or acted honestly right now?* You might be surprised by how often the consequences you fear are far less dramatic than your imagination suggests. Building self-acceptance takes time and practice, but each small step toward honesty strengthens your resilience.

The Power of Authenticity

Living authentically doesn't just change your relationship with yourself—it also transforms your connections with others. When you show up as your true self, you attract people who value and respect you for who you are, not for the roles you play or the masks you wear. Authenticity creates space for deeper, more meaningful relationships.

Moreover, expressing your individuality can infuse your life with greater purpose and joy. Whether it's through art, writing, fashion, or simply the way you speak and move through the world, self-expression allows you to tap into parts of yourself that have been waiting to shine.

Practical Steps to Embrace the Real You

Ready to start? Here are a few exercises to help you explore and express your authentic self:

1. **Write Your Personal Manifesto:** Reflect on what matters most to you—your values, passions, and dreams. Create a short declaration of who you are and what you stand for. Keep it somewhere visible as a daily reminder to live in alignment with your truth.

2. **Create a Self-Portrait:** This doesn't have to be a literal drawing or painting (though it can be!). It could be a collage of images, words, and symbols

that represent your true identity. Use it as a visual affirmation of the real you.

3. **Try One Authentic Action Per Day:** Commit to doing one thing each day that feels true to you. It could be wearing an outfit you love, sharing an honest opinion, or simply allowing yourself to rest when you're tired.

4. **Reflect on Your Wins:** Each evening, jot down one moment where you honored your authentic self that day. Celebrate these small victories—they're the foundation of lasting change.

Conclusion

Staying Strong Through Life's Ups and Downs

Life has a way of surprising us when we least expect it. You might be driving to work, humming along to your favorite song, when a wave of self-doubt hits you out of nowhere. Or perhaps, after months of feeling stronger and more confident, a single conversation with your parent—or even a memory—sends you spiraling back into old feelings of guilt or inadequacy. Healing from a childhood shaped by narcissistic parenting is often like that: unpredictable, with moments of triumph intertwined with setbacks.

Take Mia's story, for example. After setting her first boundary with her mother, she felt an empowering rush of relief. For the first time, she prioritized her needs without apologizing. But just a week later, her mother's cold response left Mia questioning everything. "Did I overreact? Was it selfish of me?" she wondered. That familiar voice of self-doubt crept back in, making her feel as if all her hard work had been undone.

If this sounds familiar, know you're not alone. Moments like these don't mean you're failing—they're part of the healing process. Healing isn't a straight path with a clear finish line; it's more like a winding road. Some days, you'll feel unstoppable, and on others, you might stumble. The key is learning how to get back up, dust yourself off, and keep moving forward.

This chapter is all about helping you stay steady on that journey. We'll explore why healing isn't linear and how to make peace with the ebbs and flows of progress. You'll discover practical daily practices to build emotional strength and resilience—things like mindfulness, journaling, and creating healthy routines that work for you. We'll also talk about the power of finding supportive communities, whether that's through therapy, support groups, or connecting with others who truly understand your experiences.

Above all, this chapter will remind you of one truth: setbacks don't erase progress. Every time you choose to keep going, even after a tough day, you're proving your strength. Healing is not about perfection; it's about perseverance. Let's dive into the tools and strategies that will help you stay strong no matter what life throws your way.

Healing Isn't Always Linear

Healing is often imagined as a smooth path, a steady climb toward a brighter future. We envision a straight line, with each step bringing us closer to peace, wholeness, and emotional freedom. But for most of us, healing looks more like a winding road with unexpected turns, bumps, and detours. It's a process that ebbs and flows, and sometimes it feels like we're taking two steps forward and one step back. And that's okay. It's important to remember that healing is rarely linear, and that's perfectly normal.

You might have moments where you feel like you're finally making progress—perhaps you've learned to set healthier boundaries or have started embracing self-compassion. Then, out of nowhere, an old wound resurfaces, and suddenly, you're back to feeling the same way you did years ago—anxious, inadequate, or deeply frustrated. It's easy to feel discouraged in these moments, especially if you've been putting in the effort to heal. But these setbacks aren't signs that you're failing. They're part of the journey, and they can provide essential opportunities for growth.

Think of it like climbing a mountain. There are moments when the climb is steep and difficult, where you might stumble or lose your footing. But with every stumble, you learn more about how to maintain your balance, how to adjust your grip, and how to find your footing again. Each challenge you face on this path only strengthens you, building your resilience and your ability to handle whatever comes next. In healing, as in mountain climbing, the key is not perfection, but perseverance.

Setbacks can be frustrating, but they are also teachers. When something triggers a deep emotional response— like an unexpected confrontation with a family member, a moment when an old behavior resurfaces, or a situation that feels too familiar to the past—it's easy to interpret these moments as failures. But they're actually revealing unresolved parts of ourselves that still need attention and care. They provide a chance to reflect on what triggered that reaction and why, offering insights into the hidden emotional baggage we may still be carrying.

The psychological reasons behind setbacks are often complex. Our minds and bodies are wired to protect us, and sometimes, that means triggering old survival mechanisms when we're faced with situations that remind us of past trauma. These emotional responses are usually connected to unresolved feelings—grief, anger, shame, or fear—that have been buried for years. When these emotions resurface, it's often a sign that they're ready to be processed, understood, and healed.

For example, you might find yourself feeling overwhelmed in a situation that reminds you of how your narcissistic parent treated you. Perhaps a person in your life behaves in a way that triggers the same feelings of inadequacy or guilt you experienced as a child. This is where your past and present intersect, and the emotional response is like a flare, signaling that there's work to be done. Rather than viewing this as a setback, try to see it as a valuable opportunity to revisit that old pain and begin working through it with the tools you've gained along the way.

It's important to remind yourself that setbacks don't equate to failure. In fact, they often show how far you've come. Each time you experience a trigger or a moment of regression, you're given a chance to apply what you've learned—to recognize that old pattern, challenge it, and choose a healthier response. Every time you face a setback, you're strengthening your emotional resilience. Healing is not about avoiding setbacks; it's about learning to navigate them with more awareness and more compassion for yourself.

So, how can you process these setbacks in a healthy way? Start by acknowledging them without judgment. It's easy to fall into the trap of blaming yourself when things don't go as planned, but self-criticism will only add to your emotional burden. Instead, treat yourself with the same kindness and understanding you would offer a friend going through a tough time. Remind yourself that healing isn't a race, and there's no deadline for feeling whole again.

Here's a reflective exercise to help you navigate setbacks in your healing journey: **Journaling Prompt:** Think about a recent setback or emotional trigger you experienced. What happened in the situation? How did you feel? Were there any thoughts or beliefs that came up that might be tied to your past experiences? Write about how you can approach these triggers with more compassion in the future. What tools can you use to shift your response?

As you reflect on these experiences, ask yourself if there's a recurring pattern in the situations that trigger you. Are there specific themes or emotions that keep resurfacing? By identifying these patterns, you can begin to understand what still needs healing and bring those areas into your conscious awareness. This is an essential step in moving through the non-linear healing process—recognizing where the work is still required and approaching it with curiosity rather than self-judgment.

Daily Practices for Emotional Health

When it comes to healing from the wounds of narcissistic parenting, it's easy to get overwhelmed by the emotional work required. The process can feel like an emotional roller coaster, full of ups and downs. But amidst the chaos, one of the most powerful tools you have at your disposal is the ability to create daily habits that nurture your emotional health. Just like physical health requires regular exercise, good nutrition, and rest, emotional health requires consistent care and attention. These small, simple practices—mindfulness, gratitude journaling, physical exercise, and maintaining a healthy routine—can serve as anchors during the storm, keeping you grounded and emotionally resilient.

One of the most important things to realize as you move forward is that emotional healing doesn't happen in a vacuum. It's not about the big moments of breakthrough, but the daily, intentional choices you make that add up over time. Just as you wouldn't expect to get in shape by working out once a month, you can't expect emotional healing to happen if you only put in the effort sporadically. The magic happens in the consistency, in showing up for yourself every single day, no matter how you feel or what life throws your way. By prioritizing emotional health practices, you build the resilience and stability that can help you face the challenges ahead with more clarity, confidence, and inner peace.

Mindfulness: Staying Present in the Moment

One of the easiest yet most transformative habits to incorporate into your daily routine is mindfulness. In simple terms, mindfulness means being fully present in the moment—tuning into your thoughts, feelings, and body without judgment. For many adult children of narcissists, being in the present moment can be a challenge. You may find yourself stuck in the past, replaying painful memories or anxiously worrying about the future. But mindfulness allows you to reconnect with the here and now, breaking the cycle of rumination and anxiety that often stems from unresolved trauma.

You don't need to set aside hours for mindfulness practice. It can be as simple as taking five minutes in the morning or before bed to focus on your breath. Try this: sit comfortably, close your eyes, and take a deep breath in, holding it for a few seconds before releasing it slowly. Notice any thoughts or feelings that come up, but try not to engage with them—just observe them like clouds passing by. Doing this practice daily can help you build emotional awareness and create space between your thoughts and reactions.

Real-life example: Sarah, a woman in her late 30s who grew up in a narcissistic household, found that mindfulness was one of the most helpful tools in managing her emotional responses. She started small, practicing mindfulness during her lunch breaks at work. After a few weeks, she noticed that her anxiety levels dropped significantly, and she felt more in control of her reactions when interacting with others, especially family members who still triggered her. Mindfulness gave her the emotional space she needed to respond thoughtfully rather than react impulsively.

Gratitude Journaling: Shifting Your Focus Toward the Positive

Another incredibly effective daily habit is gratitude journaling. It's easy to focus on the negative when you've spent years living in a narcissistic environment, but shifting your focus toward what you're grateful for can create a profound change in your emotional state. Gratitude journaling involves taking a few minutes each day to write down things you're thankful for—big or small. It helps retrain your brain to seek out the positive, even on tough days.

The key is consistency. It doesn't matter if you write three things or ten things each day, as long as you make it a habit. On days when your inner critic is loud, gratitude journaling serves as a reminder of the goodness in your life. Over time, you'll start to notice that your overall mood improves, and you begin to see the world through a more balanced lens.

Practical tip: Try to be specific when you write in your gratitude journal. Instead of just writing "I'm grateful for my family," you might write, "I'm grateful for the support my friend gave me today when I was feeling overwhelmed." This kind of detail brings more richness and authenticity to your practice.

Reflective exercise: If you've never tried gratitude journaling before, start small. Tonight, before you go to bed, write down three things you're thankful for. They could be as simple as enjoying a cup of coffee in the morning or hearing a kind word from a colleague. As you continue this practice, notice how your outlook starts to shift.

Physical Exercise: Nourishing Your Body, Healing Your Mind

Physical exercise is not just about strengthening your body—it also plays a crucial role in maintaining emotional health. When we exercise, our brains release endorphins—those feel-good chemicals that boost our mood and reduce stress. For people recovering from the emotional fallout of narcissistic parenting, exercise can serve as a way to release pent-up emotions and frustration. It can also be a way to reconnect with your body, which may have felt disconnected during years of emotional neglect or manipulation.

You don't have to be a gym enthusiast to benefit from physical exercise. Whether it's going for a walk, practicing yoga, dancing, or even stretching at home, the key is to make movement a regular part of your life. Find an activity that feels good to you—something you look forward to rather than dread. Consistency is more important than intensity. A 20-minute walk every day is far more effective than one intense workout a week.

Real-life example: Tom, a man in his 40s who spent years trying to navigate the emotional turbulence of his narcissistic upbringing, found that daily walks had an incredible impact on his mental health. Not only did the walks help him clear his mind, but they also provided a peaceful time to reflect on his feelings. Eventually, he noticed that his anxiety decreased, and his overall mood lifted.

Creating Your Personal Daily Routine

The secret to incorporating these habits into your life is to make them a non-negotiable part of your daily routine. In the hustle and bustle of life, it can be easy to let self-care slip through the cracks. But the more you prioritize these emotional health habits, the more naturally they'll become ingrained in your day. The goal isn't perfection—it's consistency.

Practical tip: Set aside specific times each day for your emotional health practices. Maybe you start your day with five minutes of mindfulness, take a gratitude break during lunch, and end your day with a short exercise session. When you make these practices part of your routine, you begin to build a foundation of emotional resilience that can withstand life's ups and downs.

Reflective exercise: Create a plan for your daily emotional health routine. What habits resonate most with you? How can you start incorporating them into your day, even in small ways?

By committing to these simple but powerful practices, you lay the groundwork for lasting emotional healing. Over time, they will help you cultivate a sense of inner peace, clarity, and strength that will carry you through life's challenges. The road ahead may not always be easy, but by staying consistent with your daily emotional health practices, you'll be better equipped to handle whatever comes your way.

Finding Your People

Healing from the wounds of narcissistic parenting is a deeply personal journey, one that often feels isolating. But as you move forward, it's important to remember this: you don't have to walk this path alone. There's incredible power in finding your people—those who understand, uplift, and support you as you reclaim your life and build a healthier future. Imagine the strength of being surrounded by a community of individuals who get it, who offer not only their empathy but also the practical encouragement you need to keep going. One woman, Emma, discovered this after years of feeling disconnected and isolated. She had grown up with a narcissistic mother who belittled her every effort and caused her to question her worth. Emma spent years thinking that she was the only one who struggled with the aftermath of such a relationship. But after joining an online support group for adult children of narcissists, she was blown away by the connection she felt. The group's members shared stories, offered resources, and provided the kind of emotional validation Emma had never experienced. With time, she found herself learning how to speak up for herself, set boundaries, and find peace within a group that truly understood her. Her healing journey was no longer a solitary one.

This is the power of supportive communities and resources. These spaces allow you to feel heard and validated—something so many adult children of narcissists yearn for. Feeling understood is not just comforting; it's a key ingredient in your emotional recovery. When you're struggling with the pain of years of invalidation, being around people who recognize your hurt can make all the difference. These connections offer emotional support that helps you remember you're not alone. Validation from others who have walked a similar road can be the spark that ignites hope in your heart and propels you forward.

The importance of staying connected with supportive individuals and groups cannot be overstated. Isolation is often a byproduct of narcissistic abuse; after years of emotional manipulation and neglect, you might have developed a habit of shutting yourself off from others. But real healing takes place when you open up to people who are safe—those who will listen without judgment, offer encouragement without strings attached, and remind you that your feelings matter. These relationships give you a sense of belonging, which is crucial for rebuilding your self-worth and emotional resilience. When you allow yourself to connect with people who genuinely care, it can feel like a weight has been lifted from your shoulders. You'll no longer carry the burden of your pain alone.

Finding the right people to walk alongside you is not always easy, but it's worth the effort. Whether in person or online, there are countless spaces where you can find kindred spirits who understand your struggles. Start by identifying communities that focus on healing from narcissistic abuse. There are support groups for adult children of narcissists that meet in person in many cities. These groups provide a structured space where you can share your experiences, hear others' stories, and gain insights from a trained facilitator. If in-person options aren't available to you, online communities are a fantastic alternative. There are numerous forums, social media groups, and virtual meetings that cater specifically to those recovering from narcissistic family dynamics. The internet has opened up access to communities that can provide you with the support you need, no matter where you live.

When choosing a community, be mindful of the environment you're entering. Look for spaces where empathy, respect, and confidentiality are prioritized. A safe, nurturing space is one where you won't be judged or told to "just get over it." It's a place where vulnerability is met with kindness, and your pain is honored. Also, pay attention to the tone and rules of engagement in online forums. If a group feels toxic or dismissive, it's okay to leave and find a more supportive one. Your well-being is the top priority. Don't settle for relationships or spaces that don't honor your healing journey.

In addition to finding your people, it's essential to take advantage of various resources available to help you on your path. Therapy is one of the most effective tools for working through the emotional and psychological impacts of narcissistic parenting. A skilled therapist, especially one experienced in narcissistic abuse or trauma recovery, can help you unpack your experiences and develop healthy coping strategies. If therapy is out of reach financially, many communities offer low-cost options, sliding scale fees, or even free services. Support groups, both in-person and virtual, provide a sense of solidarity and guidance that is invaluable as you work through the complexities of your emotions and healing process. Beyond therapy and support groups, there are countless self-help books, podcasts, and online courses specifically designed for those recovering from narcissistic abuse. These resources offer practical advice and insights that can help you navigate your healing process with clarity and confidence.

As you assess your current support network, take a moment to reflect on the connections that are serving you well. Are there relationships that provide you with comfort, validation, and encouragement? Who in your life truly understands your struggles and supports your healing journey? Reflecting on your current relationships can also highlight areas where you might be lacking support. Maybe there's a part of you that needs to connect with others who've been through similar experiences. Perhaps you've been leaning too heavily on toxic relationships that hinder your progress. Use these reflections as a starting point to make changes. Actively seek out the people and spaces that will help you grow.

Final Reflective Exercise

Take a moment to assess your support system. Who in your life can you rely on for emotional validation? Are there any relationships that are weighing you down or preventing you from healing? Write down the names of people or groups you'd like to connect with and make a plan to reach out. Consider what qualities you need in these relationships—empathy, understanding, encouragement—and use this as a guide in your search.

Remember, healing is not a solo endeavor. By finding your people and tapping into the resources available to you, you can surround yourself with the love and support necessary to navigate this journey with strength and confidence. You deserve a community that uplifts you, and with some patience and persistence, you'll find your place in it.

www.ingramcontent.com/pod-product-compliance
Lightning Source LLC
Chambersburg PA
CBHW061626250726

48659CB00004B/1102